100 Songs in **THE** the Key of "C"

EASY CHILDREN'S FAKE BOOK

Technicolor® is the registered trademark
of the Technicolor group of companies.

ISBN 978-1-4584-1122-8

HAL•LEONARD®
CORPORATION
7777 W. BLUEMOUND RD. P.O. BOX 13819 MILWAUKEE, WI 53213

Visit Hal Leonard Online at
www.halleonard.com

THE EASY CHILDREN'S FAKE BOOK

CONTENTS

INTRODUCTION

What Is a Fake Book?

A fake book has one-line music notation consisting of melody, lyrics and chord symbols.

This lead sheet format is a "musical shorthand" which is an invaluable resource for all musicians—hobbyists to professionals.

Here's how *The Easy Children's Fake Book* differs from most standard fake books:

- All songs are in the key of C.

- Many of the melodies have been simplified.

- Only five basic chord types are used—major, minor, seventh, diminished and augmented.

- The music notation is larger for ease of reading.

In the event that you haven't used chord symbols to create accompaniment, or your experience is limited, a chord speller chart is included at the back of the book to help you get started.

Have fun!

A-TISKET A-TASKET

Traditional

Moderately

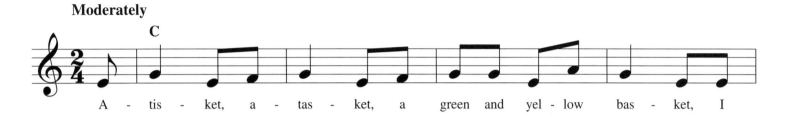

A - tis - ket, a - tas - ket, a green and yel - low bas - ket, I

wrote a let - ter to my love and on the way I dropped it. I

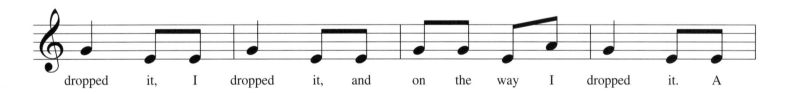

dropped it, I dropped it, and on the way I dropped it. A

lit - tle {boy}{girl} picked it up and put it in {his}{her} pock - et.

ADDAMS FAMILY THEME
Theme from the TV Show and Movie

Music and Lyrics by
VIC MIZZY

(Instrumental)

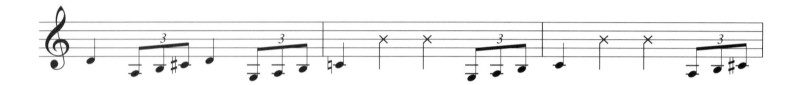

They're

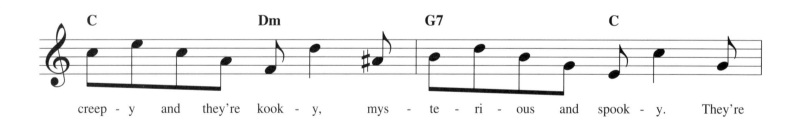

creep - y and they're kook - y, mys - te - ri - ous and spook - y. They're

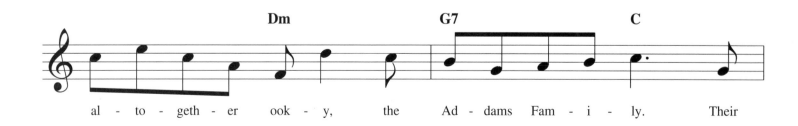

al - to - geth - er ook - y, the Ad - dams Fam - i - ly. Their

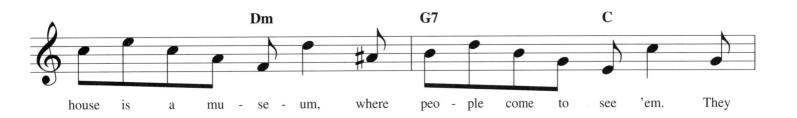

house is a mu - se - um, where peo - ple come to see 'em. They

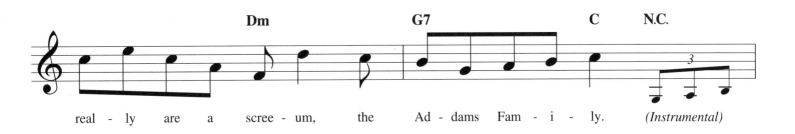

real - ly are a scree - um, the Ad - dams Fam - i - ly. *(Instrumental)*

(Spoken:) Neat.   *Sweet.*

Petite.   So get a witch -'s shawl on, a broom-stick you can crawl on. We're

gon - na pay a call on the Ad - dams Fam - i - ly.

ALL NIGHT, ALL DAY

Traditional Spiritual

Moderately

Day is dy - in' in ___ the west, an - gels watch - in' o - ver
Now I lay me down ___ to sleep, an - gels watch - in' o - ver
love stay with me through ___ the night, an - gels watch - in' o - ver

me, my Lord. ___ Sleep, my child, and take ___ your rest,
me, my Lord. ___ Pray the Lord my soul ___ to keep,
me, my Lord. ___ And wake me with the morn - ing light,

an - gels watch - in' o - ver me.
an - gels watch - in' o - ver me.
an - gels watch - in' o - ver me.

All ___ night, all ___ day,

an - gels watch - in' o - ver me, my Lord. ___ All ___ night,

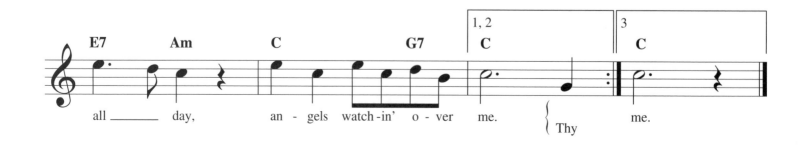

all ___ day, an - gels watch - in' o - ver me.

1, 2   3

Thy   me.

ALPHABET SONG

Traditional American School Song

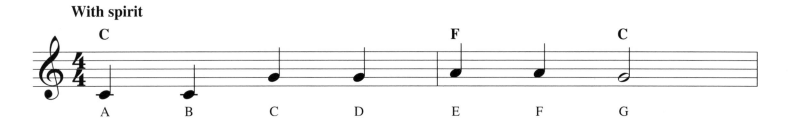

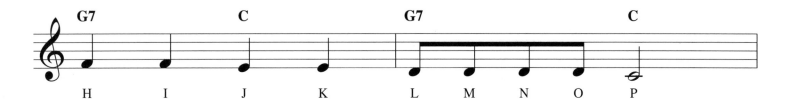

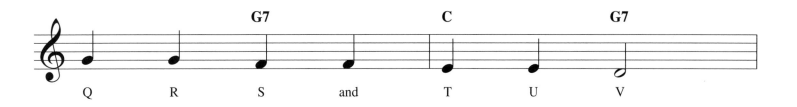

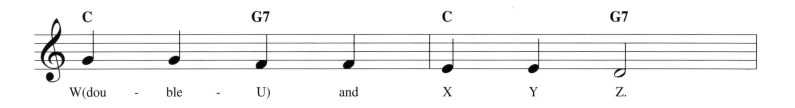

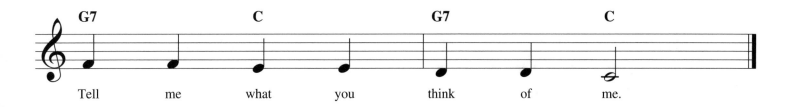

ANIMAL FAIR

American Folksong

Lightly, in 2

I went to the an - i - mal fair, _____ the birds and beasts were

there. _____ The big ba - boon, by the light of the moon, was

comb - ing his au - burn hair. _____ The mon - key, he got drunk, _____ and

sat on the el - e - phant's trunk. _____ The el - e - phant sneezed, and

fell on his knees, and what be - came of the monk, the monk, the monk, the monk?

BE KIND TO YOUR WEB-FOOTED FRIENDS

Traditional Words
Music from "The Stars and Stripes Forever"
by JOHN PHILIP SOUSA

Moderate March

Be   kind   to   your   web - foot - ed

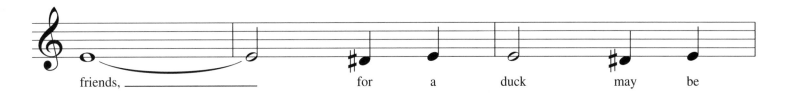

friends, _____   for   a   duck   may   be

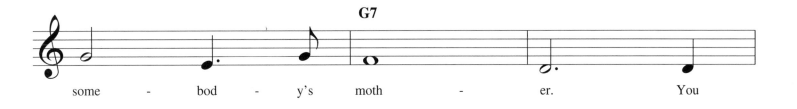

some - bod - y's   moth - er.   You

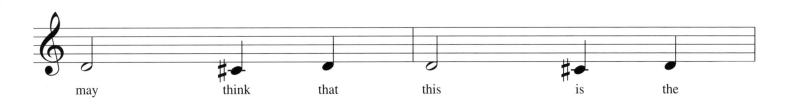

may   think   that   this   is   the

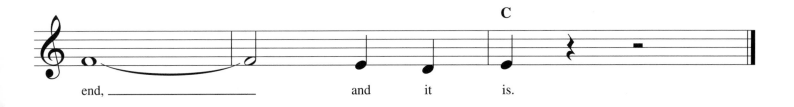

end, _____   and   it   is.

ANY DREAM WILL DO

from JOSEPH AND THE AMAZING TECHNICOLOR® DREAMCOAT

Music by ANDREW LLOYD WEBBER

Lyrics by TIM RICE

Moderately

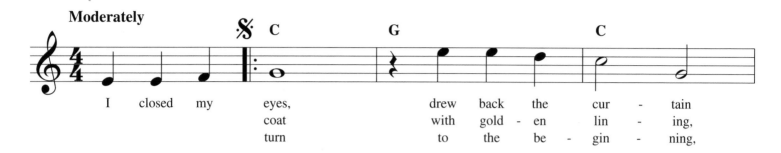

I closed my eyes, drew back the cur - tain
coat with gold - en lin - ing,
turn to the be - gin - ning,

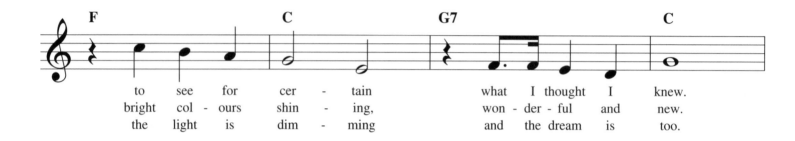

to see for cer - tain what I thought I knew.
bright col - ours shin - ing, won - der - ful and new.
the light is dim - ming and the dream is too.

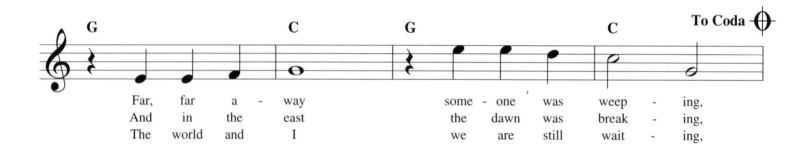

To Coda ⊕

Far, far a - way some - one was weep - ing,
And in the east the dawn was break - ing,
The world and I we are still wait - ing,

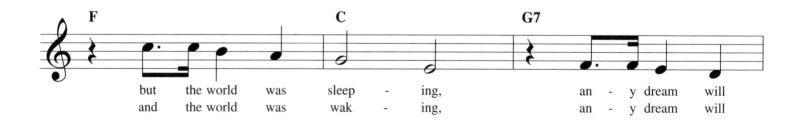

but the world was sleep - ing, an - y dream will
and the world was wak - ing, an - y dream will

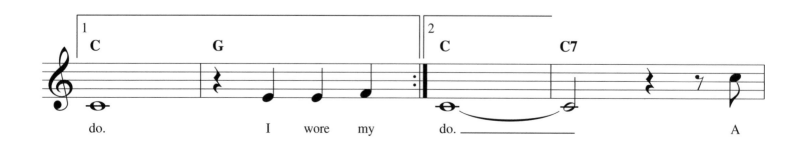

do. I wore my
do. A

crash of drums, __ a flash of light, __ my gold - en coat flew

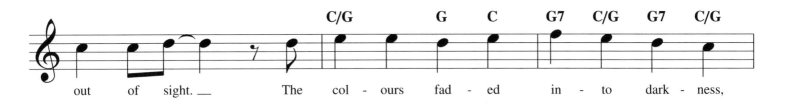

out of sight. __ The col - ours fad - ed in - to dark - ness,

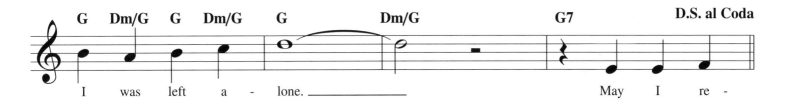

I was left a - lone. _____ May I re -

CODA

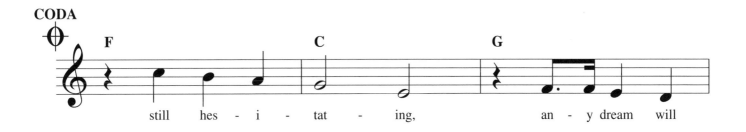

still hes - i - tat - ing, an - y dream will

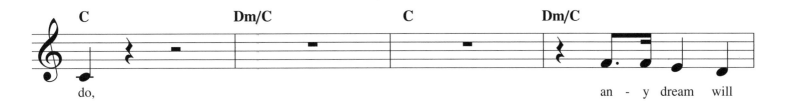

do, an - y dream will

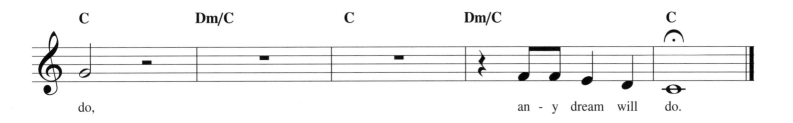

do, an - y dream will do.

THE BARE NECESSITIES
from Walt Disney's THE JUNGLE BOOK

Words and Music by
TERRY GILKYSON

With a lilt

Look for the (1.,3.) bare ne - ces - si - ties, ___ the sim - ple bare ne -
(2.) bare ne - ces - si - ties, ___ the sim - ple bare ne -

ces - si - ties; ___ for - get a - bout your wor - ries and your strife.
ces - si - ties; ___ for - get a - bout your wor - ries and your strife.

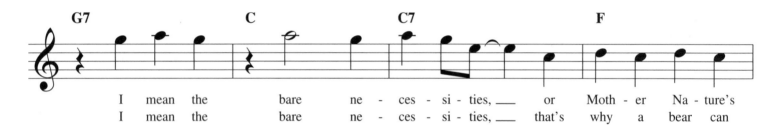

I mean the bare ne - ces - si - ties, ___ or Moth - er Na - ture's
I mean the bare ne - ces - si - ties, ___ that's why a bear can

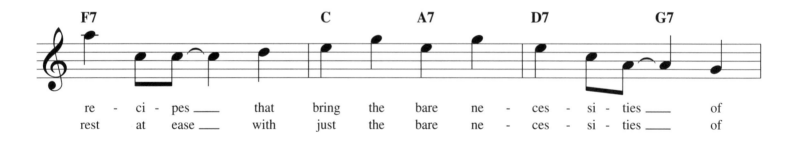

re - ci - pes ___ that bring the bare ne - ces - si - ties ___ of
rest at ease ___ with just the bare ne - ces - si - ties ___ of

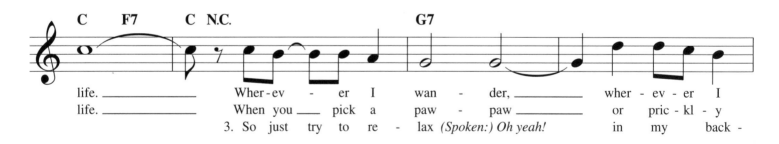

life. ___ Wher - ev - er I wan - der, ___ wher - ev - er I
life. ___ When you ___ pick a paw - paw ___ or pric - kl - y
3. So just try to re - lax (Spoken:) Oh yeah! in my back -

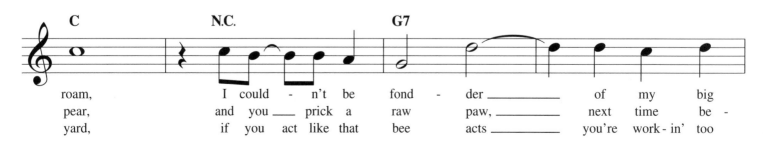

roam, I could - n't be fond - er ___ of my big
pear, and you ___ prick a raw paw, ___ next time be -
yard, if you act like that bee acts ___ you're work - in' too

THE BEAR WENT OVER THE MOUNTAIN

Traditional

Moderately

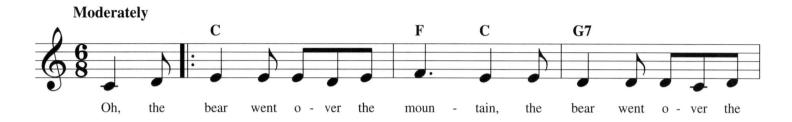

Oh, the bear went o - ver the moun - tain, the bear went o - ver the

moun - tain, the bear went o - ver the moun - tain to see what he could

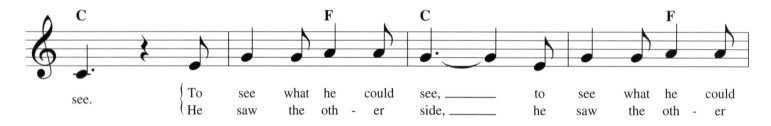

see.   To see what he could see, _____ to see what he could
He saw the oth - er side, _____ he saw the oth - er

see.   Oh, the   side.   Oh, the bear went o - ver the

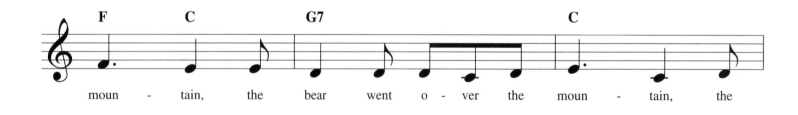

moun - tain, the bear went o - ver the moun - tain, the

bear went o - ver the moun - tain to see what he could see.

BEAUTY AND THE BEAST
from Walt Disney's BEAUTY AND THE BEAST

Lyrics by HOWARD ASHMAN
Music by ALAN MENKEN

BIBBIDI-BOBBIDI-BOO
(The Magic Song)
from Walt Disney's CINDERELLA

Words by JERRY LIVINGSTON
Music by MACK DAVID and AL HOFFMAN

Brightly

Sa - la - ga - doo - la men - chic - ka boo - la bib - bi - di - bob - bi - di - boo,

put 'em to - geth - er and what have you got? Bib - bi - di - bob - bi - di - boo.

Sa - la - ga - doo - la men - chic - ka boo - la bib - bi - di - bob - bi - di - boo,

it - 'll do mag - ic be - lieve it or not, bib - bi - di - bob - bi - di - boo. Sa - la - ga - doo - la means

men - chic - ka boo - le - roo, but the thing - a - ma - bob that does the job is

bib - bi - di - bob - bi - di - boo. Sa - la - ga - doo - la men - chic - ka boo - la

bib - bi - di - bob - bi - di - boo, put 'em to - geth - er and what have you got?

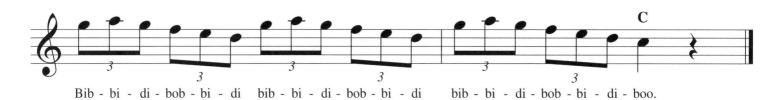

Bib - bi - di - bob - bi - di bib - bi - di - bob - bi - di bib - bi - di - bob - bi - di - boo.

A BICYCLE BUILT FOR TWO
(Daisy Bell)

Words and Music by
HARRY DACRE

Moderate Waltz

THE BIBLE TELLS ME SO

Words and Music by
DALE EVANS

Moderately

Have faith, hope and char - i - ty, ____ that's the way to live suc -

cess - ful - ly. ____ How do I know? The Bi - ble tells me

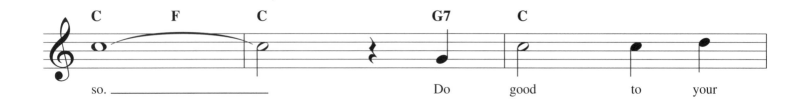

so. _____ Do good to your

en - e - mies ____ and the Bless - ed Lord you'll sure - ly please. _

How do I know? The Bi - ble tells me so. _____

21

Don't wor - ry 'bout to - mor - row, just

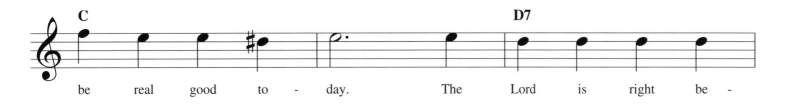

be real good to - day. The Lord is right be -

side you, He'll guide you all the way. Have

faith, hope and char - i - ty, _____ that's the way to live suc -

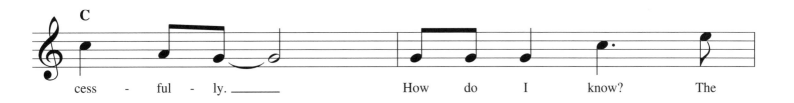

cess - ful - ly. _____ How do I know? The

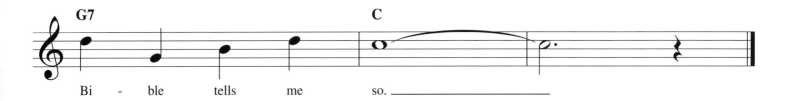

Bi - ble tells me so. _____

BINGO

18th Century English Game Song

Note: Each time a letter of BINGO is deleted
in the lyric, clap your hands in place of singing the letter.

There was a farm-er had a dog and Bin-go was his name - o.

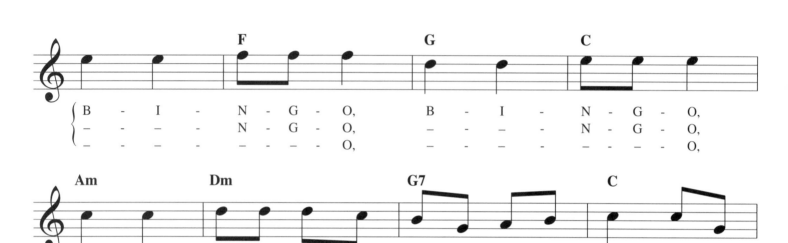

B - I - N - G - O, B - I - N - G - O,
— - — - N - G - O, — - — - — - N - G - O,
— - — - — - — - — - O, — - — - — - — - — - O,

B - I - N - G - O } and Bin-go was his name - o. There
— - — - — - N - G - O }
— - — - — - — - — - O }

was a farm-er had a dog and Bin-go was his name - o.

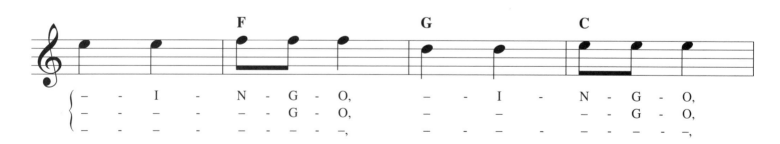

{ — - — - I - N - G - O, — - — - I - N - G - O,
{ — - — - — - — - G - O, — - — - — - — - G - O,
{ — - — - — - — - — -, — - — - — - — - — -,

— - I - N - G - O } and Bin-go was his name. There name - o.
— - — - — - G - O }
— - — - — - — - — -,

THE BLUE TAIL FLY
(Jimmy Crack Corn)

Words and Music by
DANIEL DECATUR EMMETT

Lively

1. When I was young, I used to wait on mas - ter, hand - ing him his plate. I
2. He used to ride each af - ter - noon, I'd fol - low with a hick - 'ry broom. The
3. The po - ny jump, he run, he pitch, he threw my mas - ter in the ditch. My

4., 5. *(See additional lyrics)*

brought his bot - tle when he was dry and brushed a - way the blue - tail fly.
po - ny kicked his legs up high, when bit - ten by the blue - tail fly.
mas - ter died and who'll de - ny, the blame was on the blue - tail fly.

Chorus

Jim - my crack corn and I don't care, Jim - my crack corn and I don't care,

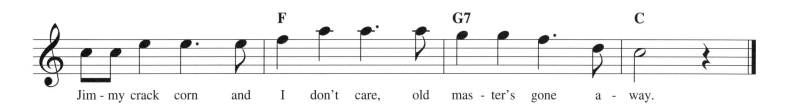

Jim - my crack corn and I don't care, old mas - ter's gone a - way.

Additional Lyrics

4. Old master's dead and gone to rest,
   They say it happened for the best.
   I won't forget until I die
   My master and the blue-tail fly.
   Chorus

5. A skeeter bites right through your clothes,
   A hornet strikes you on the nose,
   The bees may get you passing by,
   But, oh, much worse, the blue-tail fly.
   Chorus

BOB THE BUILDER "INTRO THEME SONG"

Words and Music by
PAUL JOYCE

Moderately fast

Bob the Build-er. (Can we fix it?) Bob the Build-er. (Yes, we can!)

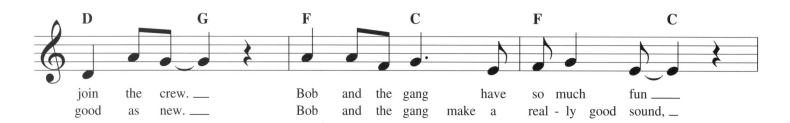

Scoop, Block and Diz-zy and Ro-ly, too; ___ Lof-ty and Wen-dy
Time to get bus-y; such a lot to do, ___ build-ing and fix-ing 'til it's

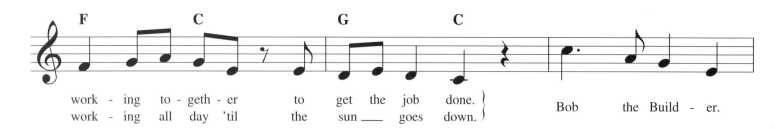

join the crew. ___ Bob and the gang have so much fun ___
good as new. ___ Bob and the gang make a real-ly good sound, ___

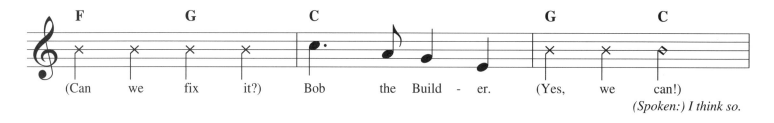

work-ing to-geth-er to get the job done.
work-ing all day 'til the sun ___ goes down. } Bob the Build-er.

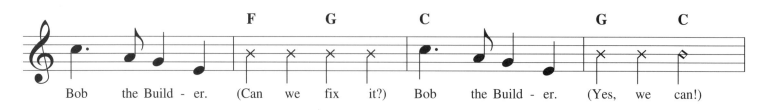

(Can we fix it?) Bob the Build-er. (Yes, we can!)

(Spoken:) I think so.

Bob the Build-er. (Can we fix it?) Bob the Build-er. (Yes, we can!)

(Instrumental)

BUFFALO GALS
(Won't You Come Out Tonight?)

Words and Music by
COOL WHITE (JOHN HODGES)

With motion

Buf - fa - lo gals, won't ya come out to - night, won't ya come out to - night, won't ya
Yes, pret - ty boys, we'll come out to - night, we'll come out to - night, we'll

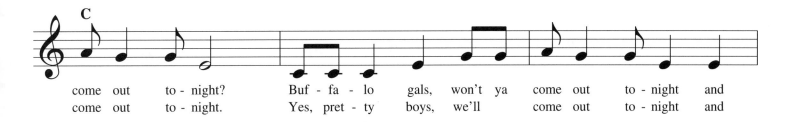

come out to - night? Buf - fa - lo gals, won't ya come out to - night and
come out to - night. Yes, pret - ty boys, we'll come out to - night and

dance by the light of the moon? I danced with a gal with a
dance by the light of the moon.

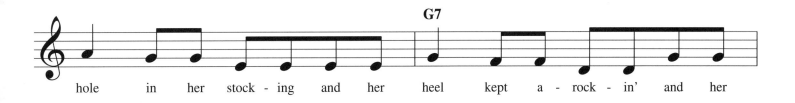

hole in her stock - ing and her heel kept a - rock - in' and her

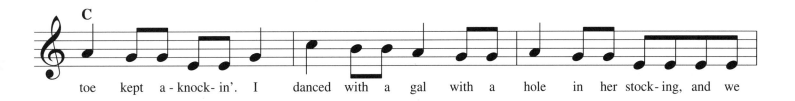

toe kept a - knock - in'. I danced with a gal with a hole in her stock - ing, and we

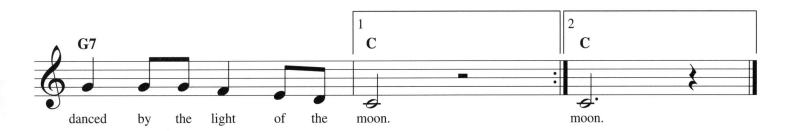

1.
danced by the light of the moon.

2.
moon.

THE BRADY BUNCH
Theme from the Paramount Television Series THE BRADY BUNCH

Words and Music by SHERWOOD SCHWARTZ
and FRANK DEVOL

Happily, in 2

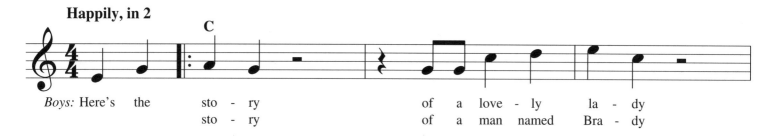

Boys: Here's the sto - ry of a love - ly la - dy
sto - ry of a man named Bra - dy

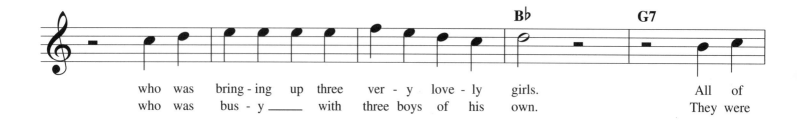

who was bring - ing up three ver - y love - ly girls. All of
who was bus - y with three boys of his own. They were

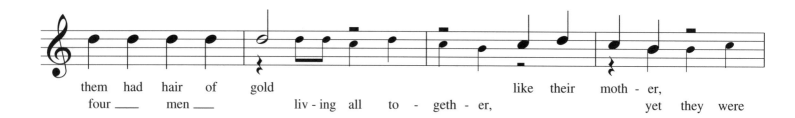

them had hair of gold like their moth - er,
four men liv - ing all to - geth - er, yet they were

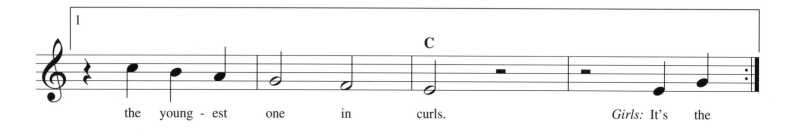

the young - est one in curls. *Girls:* It's the

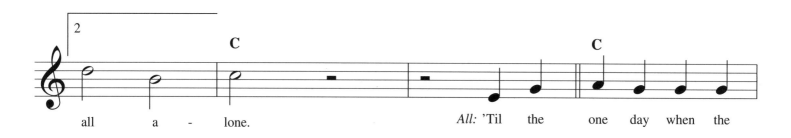

all a - lone. *All:* 'Til the one day when the

la - dy met this fel - low, and they knew that it was

29

much more than a hunch that this group must

some - how form a fam - 'ly. That's the way we all be -

came the Bra - dy Bunch. The Bra - dy Bunch,

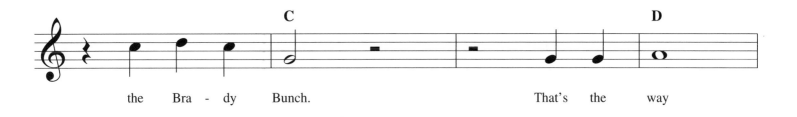

the Bra - dy Bunch. That's the way

we be - came the Bra - dy Bunch. *(Instrumental)*

"C" IS FOR COOKIE

Words and Music by
JOE RAPOSO

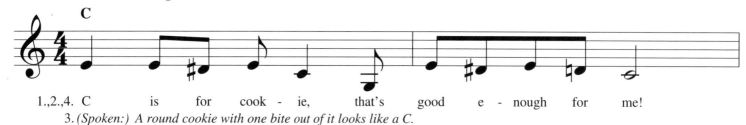

1.,2.,4. C   is   for   cook - ie,   that's   good   e - nough   for   me!
3. *(Spoken:) A round cookie with one bite out of it looks like a C.*

C   is   for   cook - ie,   that's   good   e - nough   for   me!
A round doughnut with one bite out of it looks like a C,

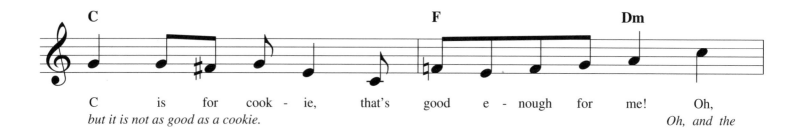

C   is   for   cook - ie,   that's   good   e - nough   for   me!   Oh,
but it is not as good as a cookie.   *Oh,   and the*

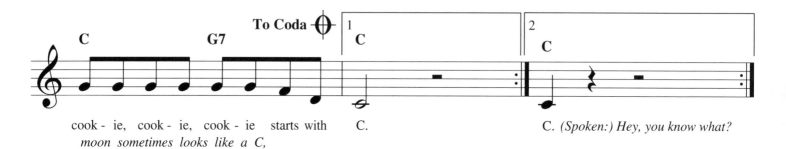

cook - ie,   cook - ie,   cook - ie   starts   with   C.   C. *(Spoken:) Hey, you know what?*
moon   sometimes   looks   like   a   C,

but you can't eat that.   So   C.   Yeah!   Cook - ie,   cook - ie,   cook - ie   starts   with

C.   Oh boy!   Cook - ie,   cook - ie,   cook - ie   starts   with   C.

CLAP YOUR HANDS

Words and Music by JIMMY OWENS
and CAROL OWENS

Joyfully

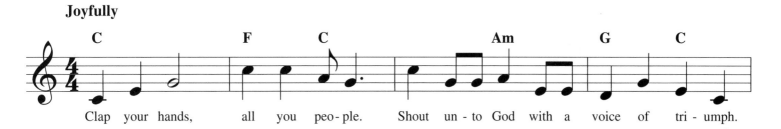

Clap your hands, all you peo-ple. Shout un-to God with a voice of tri - umph.

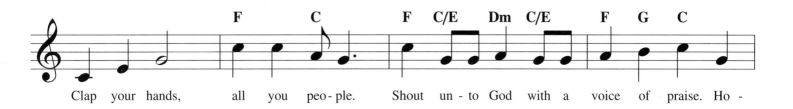

Clap your hands, all you peo-ple. Shout un-to God with a voice of praise. Ho -

san - na! Ho-san - na! Shout un-to God with a voice of tri - umph.

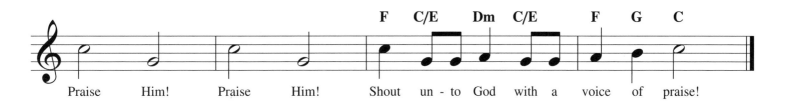

Praise Him! Praise Him! Shout un-to God with a voice of praise!

CANDLE ON THE WATER
from Walt Disney's PETE'S DRAGON

Words and Music by AL KASHA
and JOEL HIRSCHHORN

Smoothly

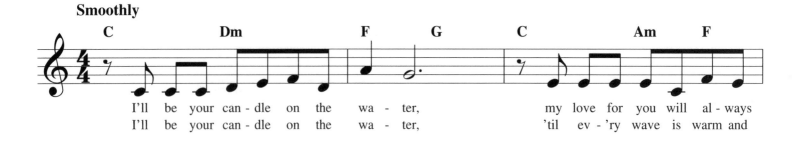

I'll be your can-dle on the wa-ter, my love for you will al-ways
I'll be your can-dle on the wa-ter, 'til ev-'ry wave is warm and

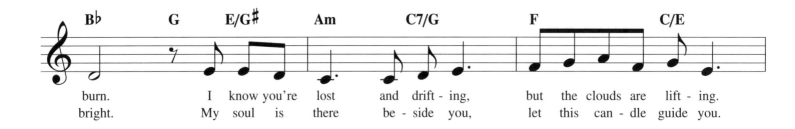

burn. I know you're lost and drift-ing, but the clouds are lift-ing.
bright. My soul is there be-side you, let this can-dle guide you.

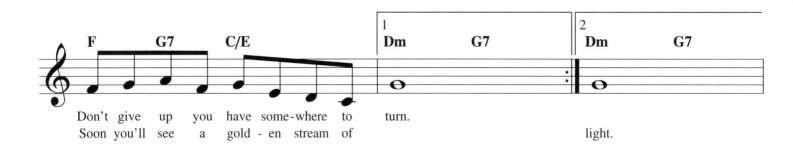

Don't give up you have some-where to turn.
Soon you'll see a gold-en stream of light.

A cold and friend-less tide has found you, don't let the storm-y dark-ness

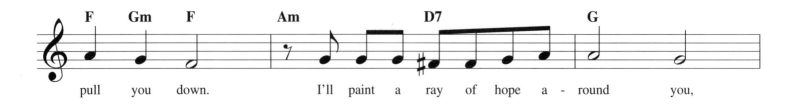

pull you down. I'll paint a ray of hope a-round you,

cir-cling in the air light-ed by a prayer.

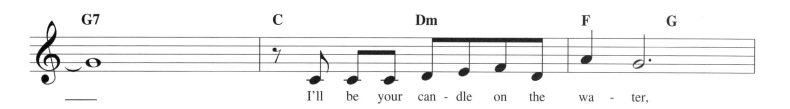

I'll be your can - dle on the wa - ter,

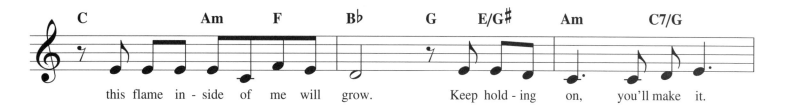

this flame in - side of me will grow. Keep hold - ing on, you'll make it.

Here's my hand so take it, look for me reach - ing out to show as sure as riv - ers

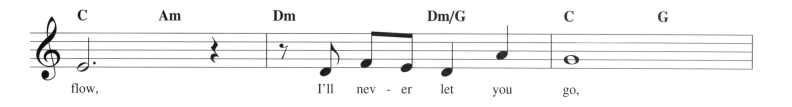

flow, I'll nev - er let you go,

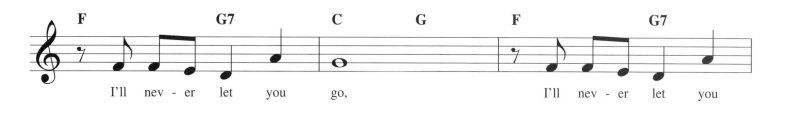

I'll nev - er let you go, I'll nev - er let you

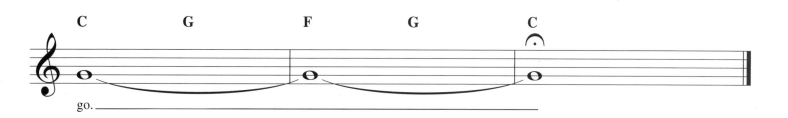

go.

THE CANDY MAN
from WILLY WONKA AND THE CHOCOLATE FACTORY

Words and Music by LESLIE BRICUSSE
and ANTHONY NEWLEY

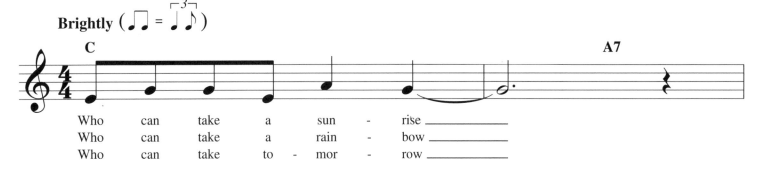

Who can take a sun - rise
Who can take a rain - bow
Who can take to - mor - row

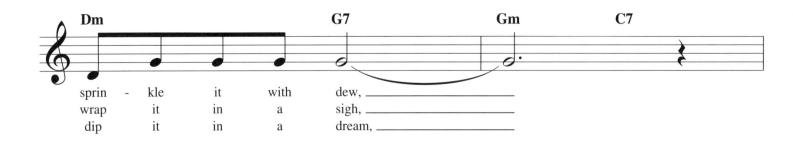

sprin - kle it with dew,
wrap it in a sigh,
dip it in a dream,

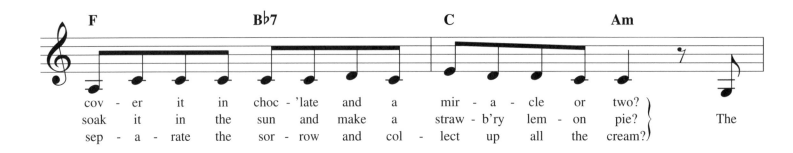

cov - er it in choc - 'late and a mir - a - cle or two? } The
soak it in the sun and make a straw - b'ry lem - on pie? }
sep - a - rate the sor - row and col - lect up all the cream? }

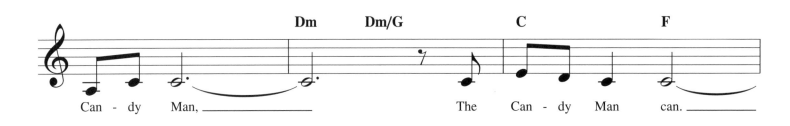

Can - dy Man, The Can - dy Man can.

The Can - dy Man can 'cause he

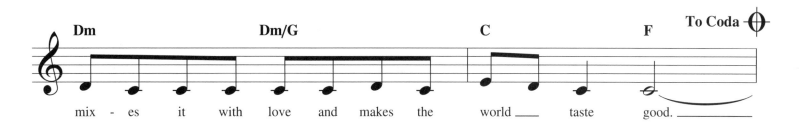

mix - es it with love and makes the world ___ taste good. ___

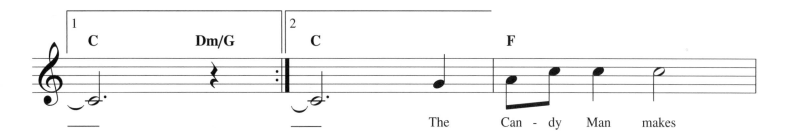

___   ___   The Can - dy Man makes

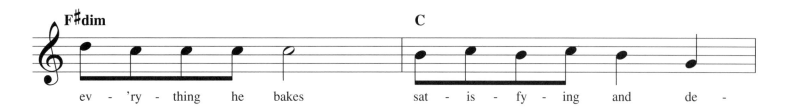

ev - 'ry - thing he bakes   sat - is - fy - ing and de -

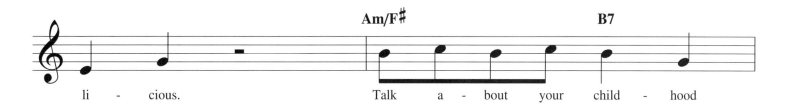

li - cious.   Talk a - bout your child - hood

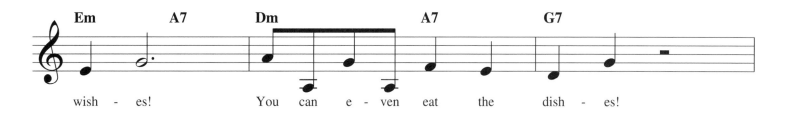

wish - es!   You can e - ven eat the dish - es!

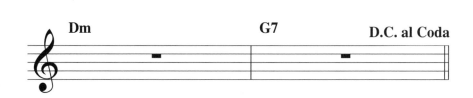

D.C. al Coda

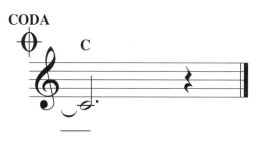

CODA

(Oh, My Darling)
CLEMENTINE

Words and Music by
PERCY MONTROSE

Moderately

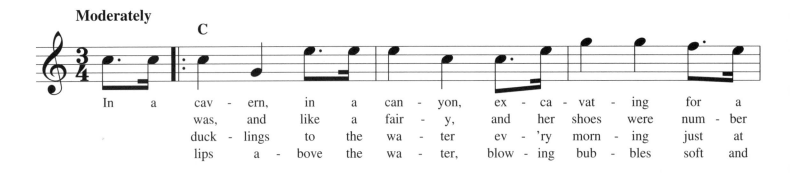

In a cav - ern, in a can - yon, ex - ca - vat - ing for a
was, and like a fair - y, and her shoes were num - ber
duck - lings to the wa - ter ev - 'ry morn - ing just at
lips a - bove the wa - ter, blow - ing bub - bles soft and

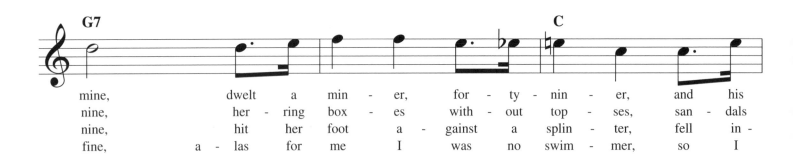

mine, dwelt a min - er, for - ty - nin - er, and his
nine, her - ring box - es with - out top - ses, san - dals
nine, hit her foot a - gainst a splin - ter, fell in -
fine, a - las for me I was no swim - mer, so I

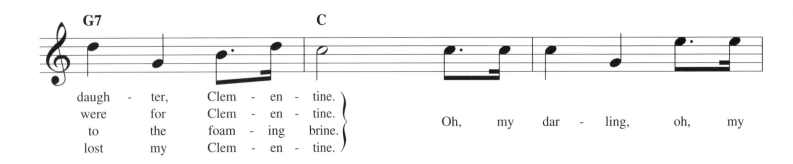

daugh - ter, Clem - en - tine.
were for Clem - en - tine.
to the foam - ing brine.
lost my Clem - en - tine.

Oh, my dar - ling, oh, my

dar - ling, oh, my dar - ling, Clem - en - tine, you are lost and gone for-

ev - er. Dread - ful sor - ry, Clem - en - tine.

Light she
Drove she   tine.
Ru - by

DO-RE-MI

from THE SOUND OF MUSIC

Lyrics by OSCAR HAMMERSTEIN II
Music by RICHARD RODGERS

DOWN BY THE STATION

Traditional

Steadily

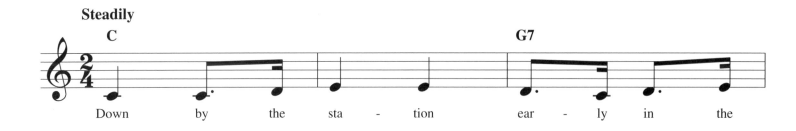

Down by the sta - tion ear - ly in the

morn - ing, see the lit - tle puf - fer - bil - lies

all in a row. See the en - gine

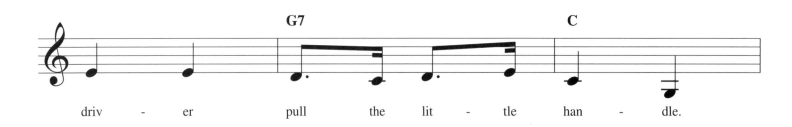

driv - er pull the lit - tle han - dle.

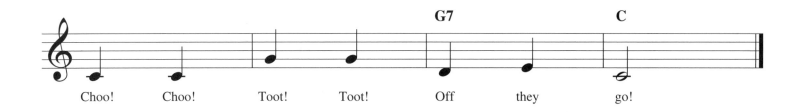

Choo! Choo! Toot! Toot! Off they go!

EDELWEISS
from THE SOUND OF MUSIC

Lyrics by OSCAR HAMMERSTEIN II
Music by RICHARD RODGERS

Moderately

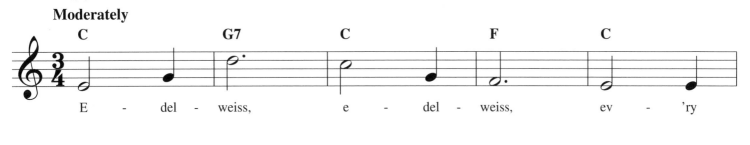

E - del - weiss, e - del - weiss, ev - 'ry

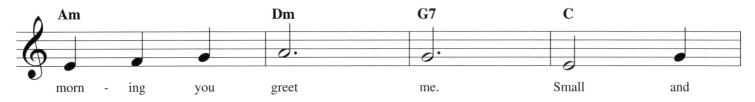

morn - ing you greet me. Small and

white, clean and bright, you look hap - py to

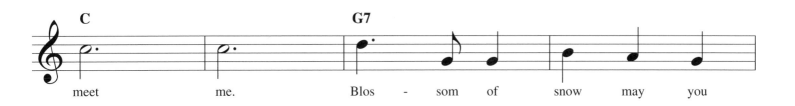

meet me. Blos - som of snow may you

bloom and grow, bloom and grow for - ev -

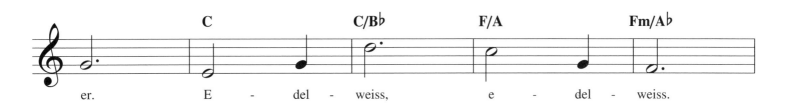

er. E - del - weiss, e - del - weiss.

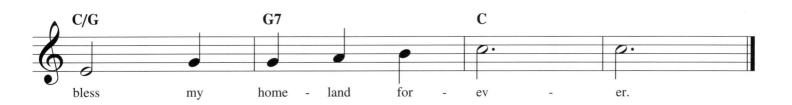

bless my home - land for - ev - er.

EENSY, WEENSY SPIDER

Traditional

Moderately

Een - sy, ween - sy spi - der went up the wa - ter -

spout. Down came the rain and washed the spi - der

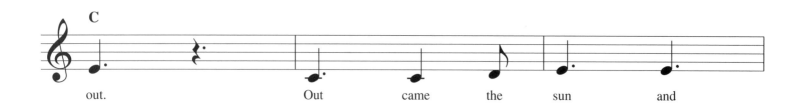

out. Out came the sun and

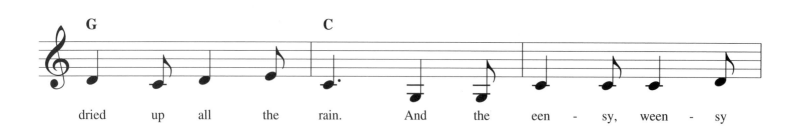

dried up all the rain. And the een - sy, ween - sy

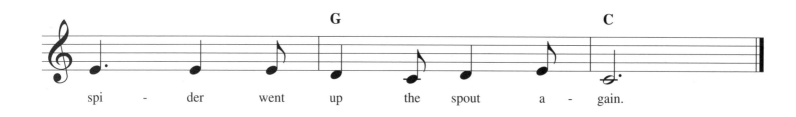

spi - der went up the spout a - gain.

FOR HE'S A JOLLY GOOD FELLOW

Traditional

ELMO'S SONG

Words and Music by
TONY GEISS

This is the song, la la la la, El - mo's song.

La la la la, la la la la,

El - mo's song. La la la la la la

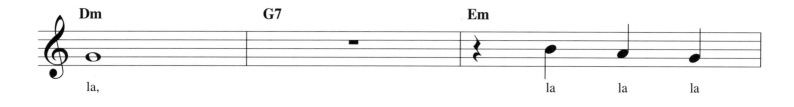

la, la la la

la la la la.

43

He loves to sing, la la la la, El - mo's song.

La la la la, la la la la,

El - mo's song. He wrote the

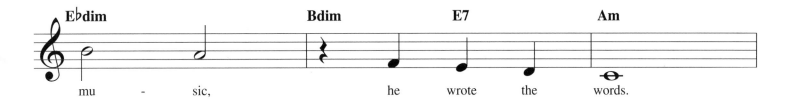

mu - sic, he wrote the words.

That's El - mo's song.

FRÈRE JACQUES
(Are You Sleeping?)

Traditional

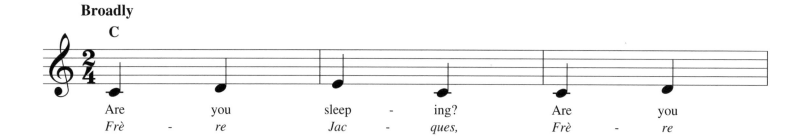

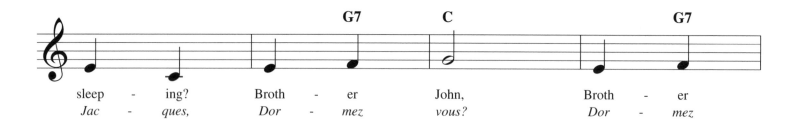

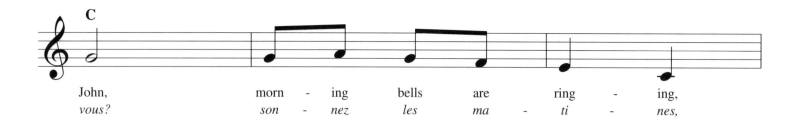

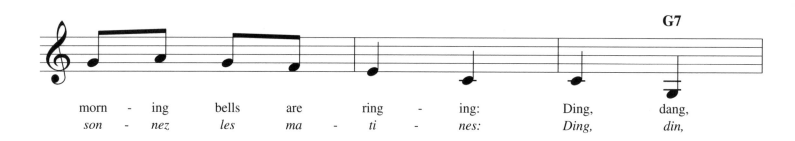

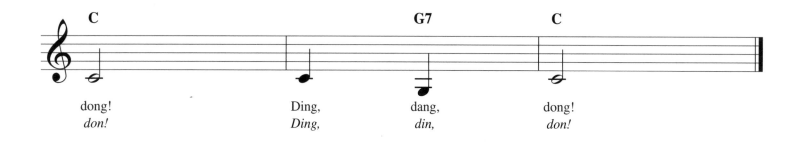

HAKUNA MATATA
from Walt Disney Pictures' THE LION KING

Music by ELTON JOHN
Lyrics by TIM RICE

Freely

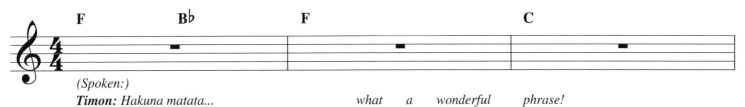

(Spoken:)
Timon: Hakuna matata...   *what   a   wonderful   phrase!*

Pumbaa: Hakuna matata...   ain't   no   pass - ing

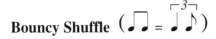

Bouncy Shuffle

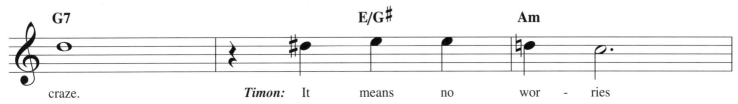

craze.   *Timon:* It   means   no   wor - ries

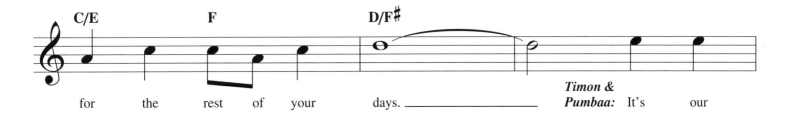

for   the   rest   of   your   days. _____   *Timon &*
Pumbaa: It's   our

prob - lem - free _____   phi - los - o - phy.

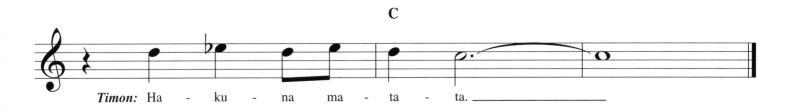

Timon: Ha - ku - na   ma - ta - ta. _____

GETTING TO KNOW YOU

from THE KING AND I

Lyrics by OSCAR HAMMERSTEIN II
Music by RICHARD RODGERS

Moderately

Get - ting to know you, get - ting to know all a -

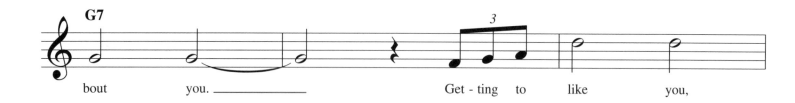

bout you. Get - ting to like you,

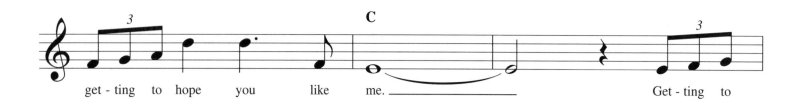

get - ting to hope you like me. Get - ting to

know you, put - ting it my way but nice - ly,

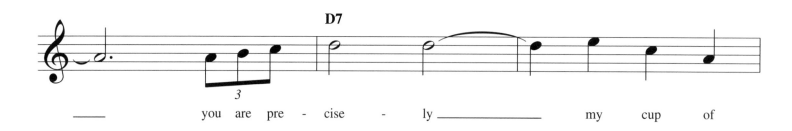

you are pre - cise - ly my cup of

tea. Get - ting to know you,

47

get - ting to feel free and eas - y. _____ When I am

with you, get - ting to know what to say. _____

_____ Have - n't you no - ticed, sud - den - ly I'm bright and

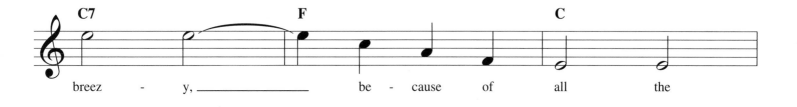

breez - y, _____ be - cause of all the

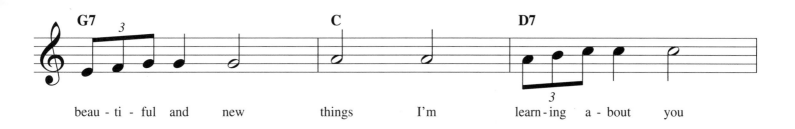

beau - ti - ful and new things I'm learn - ing a - bout you

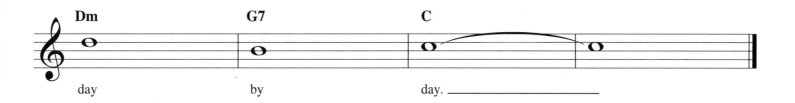

day by day. _____

HAPPY TRAILS
from the Television Series THE ROY ROGERS SHOW

Words and Music by
DALE EVANS

HE'S GOT THE WHOLE WORLD IN HIS HANDS

Traditional Spiritual

HEART AND SOUL
from the Paramount Short Subject A SONG IS BORN

Words by FRANK LOESSER
Music by HOAGY CARMICHAEL

Moderately

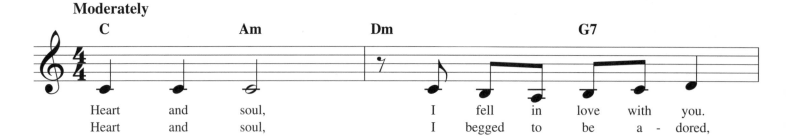

Heart and soul, I fell in love with you.
Heart and soul, I begged to be a - dored,

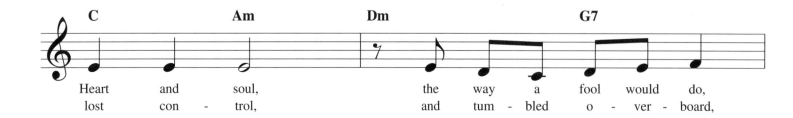

Heart and soul, the way a fool would do,
lost con - trol, and tum - bled o - ver - board,

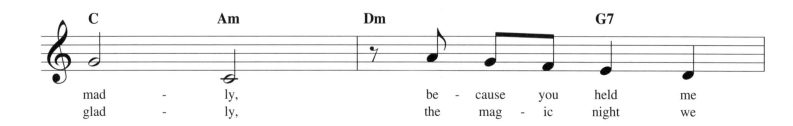

mad - ly, be - cause you held me
glad - ly, the mag - ic night we

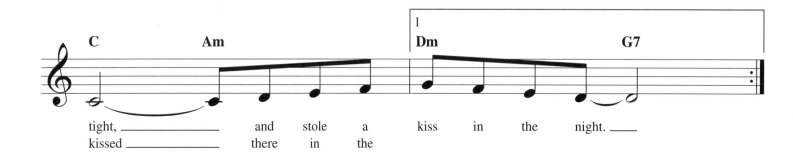

tight, _____ and stole a kiss in the night. ____
kissed _____ there in the

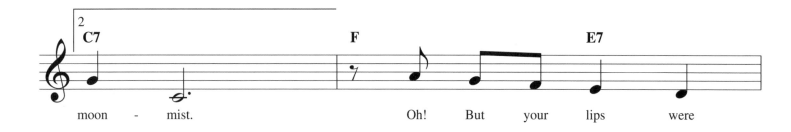

moon - mist. Oh! But your lips were

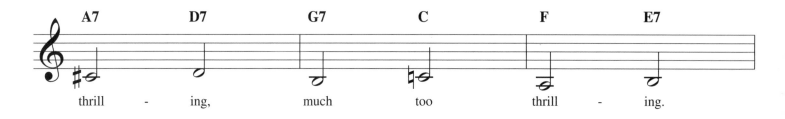

thrill - ing, much too thrill - ing.

51

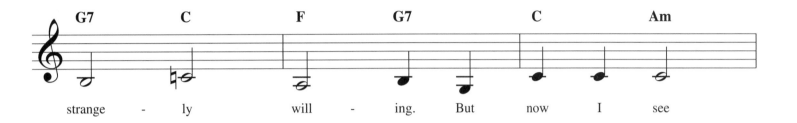

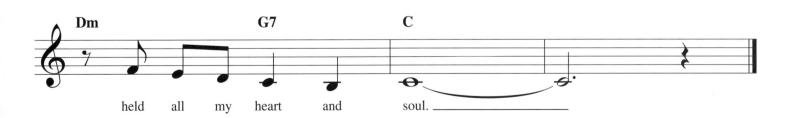

HOME ON THE RANGE

Lyrics by DR. BREWSTER HIGLEY
Music by DAN KELLY

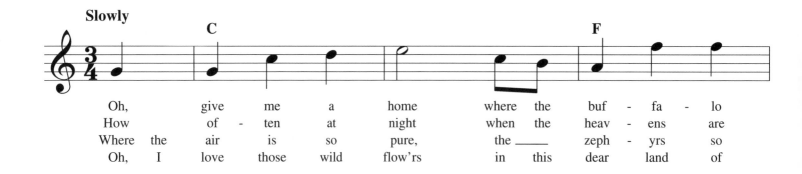

Oh,   give   me   a   home   where   the   buf - fa - lo
How   of - ten   at   night   when   the   heav - ens   are
Where   the   air   is   so   pure,   the ____ zeph - yrs   so
Oh,   I   love   those   wild   flow'rs   in   this   dear   land   of

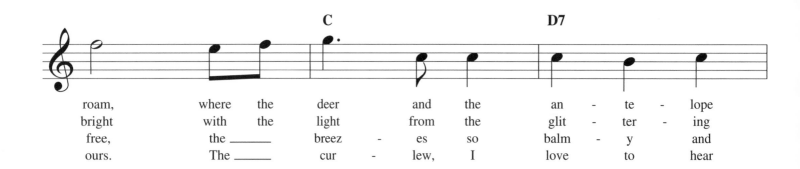

roam,   where   the   deer   and   the   an - te - lope
bright   with   the   light   from   the   glit - ter - ing
free,   the ____ breez - es   so   balm - y   and
ours.   The ____ cur - lew,   I   love   to   hear

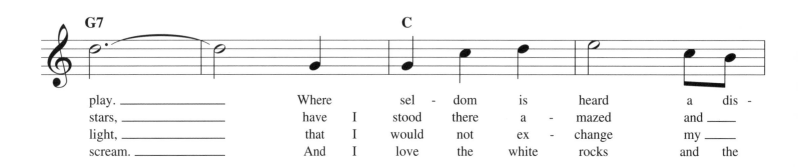

play. _____   Where   sel - dom   is   heard   a   dis-
stars, _____   have   I   stood   there   a - mazed   and ____
light, _____   that   I   would   not   ex - change   my ____
scream. _____   And   I   love   the   white   rocks   and   the

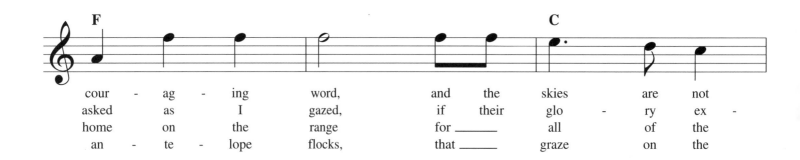

cour - ag - ing   word,   and   the   skies   are   not
asked   as   I   gazed,   if   their   glo - ry   ex-
home   on   the   range   for ____ all   of   the
an - te - lope   flocks,   that ____ graze   on   the

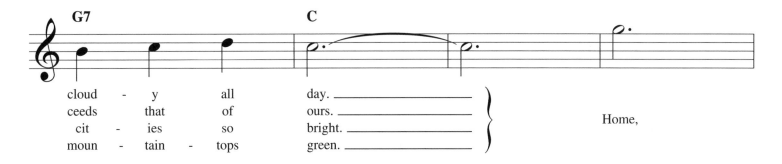

cloud - y all day. _____
ceeds that of ours. _____
cit - ies so bright. _____
moun - tain - tops green. _____

Home,

home on the range, _____ where the deer and the

an - te - lope play. _____ Where sel - dom is

heard a dis - cour - ag - ing word, and the

skies are not cloud - y all day. _____

HOW MUCH IS THAT DOGGIE IN THE WINDOW

Words and Music by
BOB MERRILL

Moderately

How much is that dog - gie in the win - dow? _____ The

one with the wag - gle - y tail. _____ How

much is that dog - gie in the win - dow? _____ I

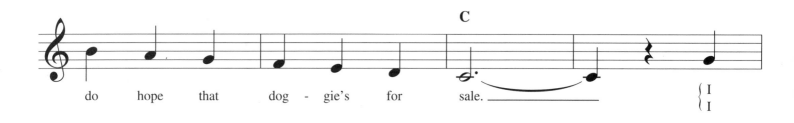

do hope that dog - gie's for sale. _____
{ I
{ I

must take a trip to Cal - i - for - nia _____ and
read in the pa - pers there are rob - bers _____ with

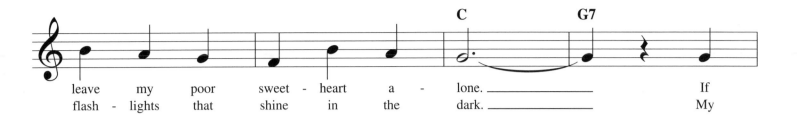

leave my poor sweet - heart a - lone. _____ If
flash - lights that shine in the dark. _____ My

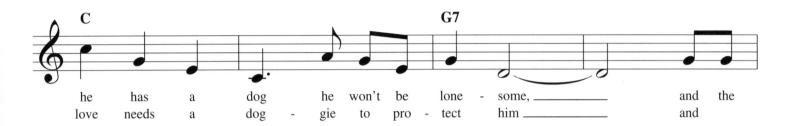

he has a dog he won't be lone - some, _____ and the
love needs a dog - gie to pro - tect him _____ and

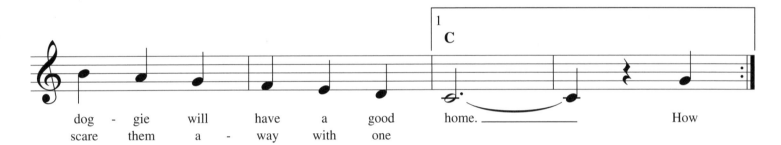

dog - gie will have a good home. _____ How
scare them a - way with one

bark. _____ I

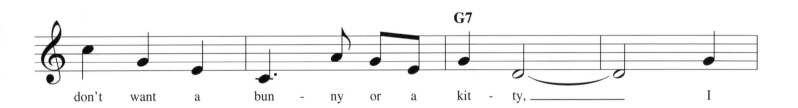

don't want a bun - ny or a kit - ty, _____ I

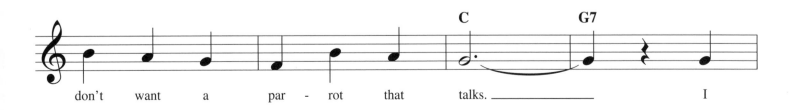

don't want a par - rot that talks. _____ I

don't want a bowl of lit - tle fish - ies; _____ he

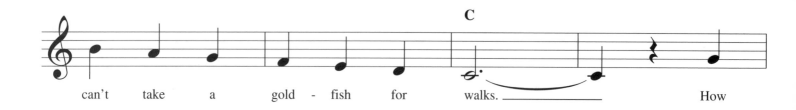

can't take a gold - fish for walks. _____ How

much is that dog - gie in the win - dow? _____ The

one with the wag - gle - y tail. _____ How

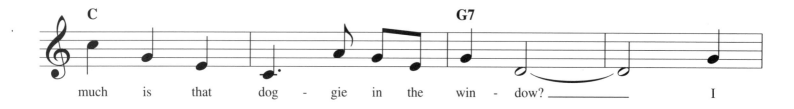

much is that dog - gie in the win - dow? _____ I

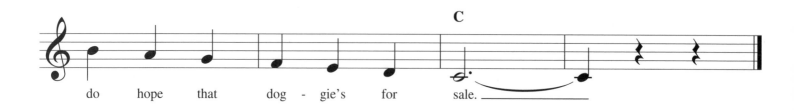

do hope that dog - gie's for sale. _____

THE HOKEY POKEY

Words and Music by CHARLES P. MACAK,
TAFFT BAKER and LARRY LaPRISE

1. You put your *right foot in, you put your *right foot out. You put your
2.-10. *(See additional lyrics)*

*right foot in, and you shake it all a-bout. You do the Hok-ey Pok-ey, and you

turn your-self a-round. That's what it's all a-bout. You do the

Hok - ey Pok - ey. _____ You do the Hok - ey

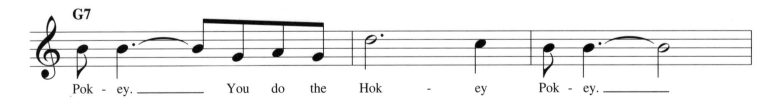

Pok - ey. _____ You do the Hok - ey Pok - ey. _____

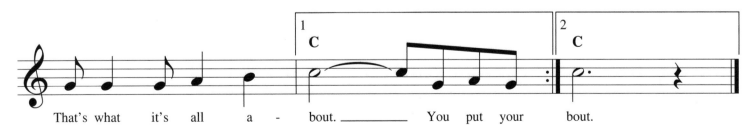

That's what it's all a-bout. _____ You put your bout.

Additional Lyrics

*2nd time: left foot
*3rd time: right arm
*4th time: left arm
*5th time: right elbow
*6th time: left elbow

*7th time: head
*8th time: right hip
*9th time: left hip
*10th time: whole self

I WHISTLE A HAPPY TUNE
from THE KING AND I

Lyrics by OSCAR HAMMERSTEIN II
Music by RICHARD RODGERS

Brightly

When - ev - er I feel a - fraid, I hold my head e -

rect and whis - tle a hap - py tune, so

no one will sus - pect I'm a - fraid._____ While

shiv - er - ing in my shoes, I strike a care - less

pose and whis - tle a hap - py tune and

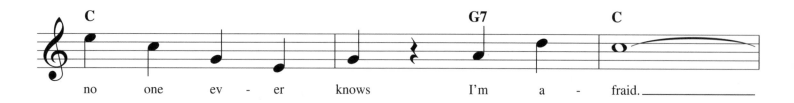

no one ev - er knows I'm a - fraid._____

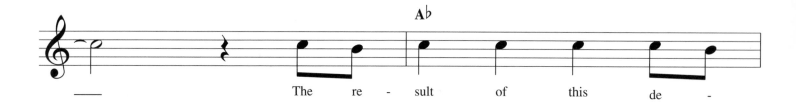

_____ The re - sult of this de -

59

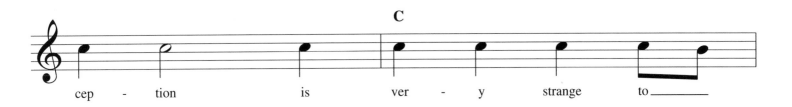

cep - tion   is   ver - y   strange   to_____

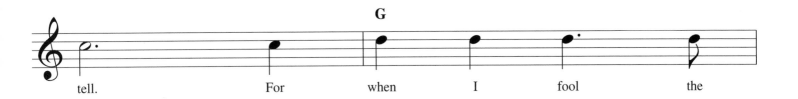

tell.   For   when   I   fool   the

peo - ple   I   fear,   I   fool   my - self   as

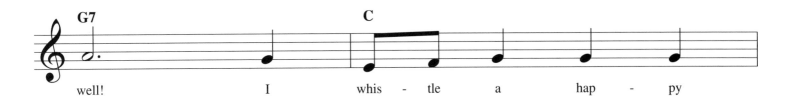

well!   I   whis - tle a   hap - py

tune   and   ev - 'ry   sin - gle   time   the

hap - pi - ness in   the   tune con - vinc - es me that

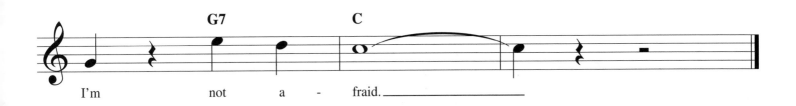

I'm   not   a - fraid._____

I'M POPEYE THE SAILOR MAN
Theme from the Paramount Cartoon POPEYE THE SAILOR

Words and Music by
SAMMY LERNER

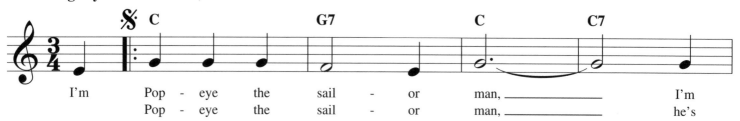

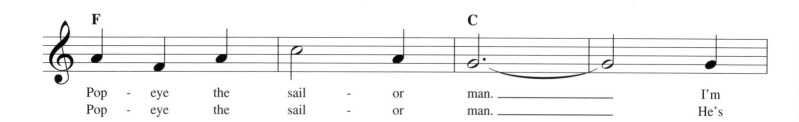

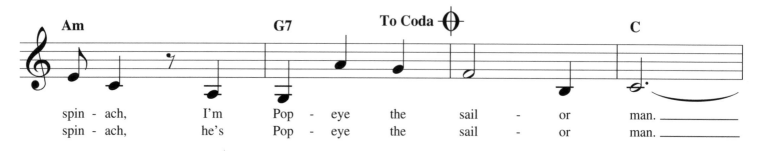

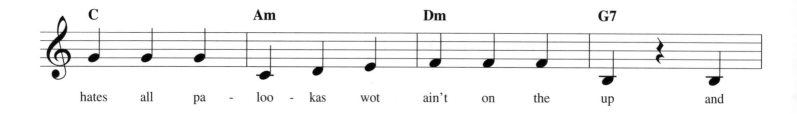

61

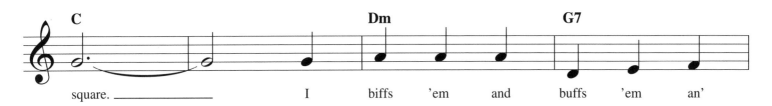

square. _____ I biffs 'em and buffs 'em an'

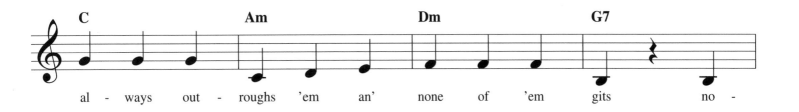

al - ways out - roughs 'em an' none of 'em gits no -

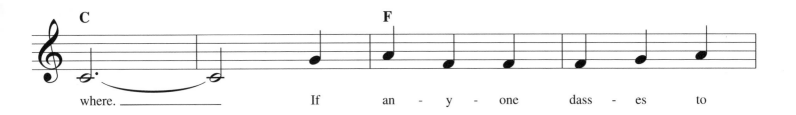

where. _____ If an - y - one dass - es to

risk my "fisk," it's "boff" an' it's "wham," un - 'er -

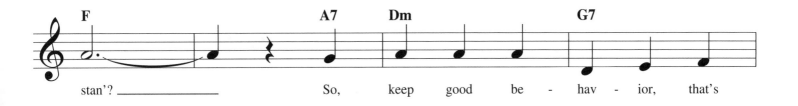

stan'? _____ So, keep good be - hav - ior, that's

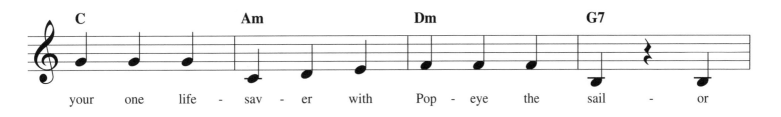

your one life - sav - er with Pop - eye the sail - or

D.S. al Coda
(with repeat)

CODA

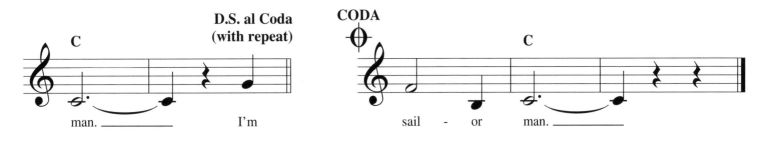

man. _____ I'm   sail - or man. _____

I'VE BEEN WORKING ON THE RAILROAD

American Folksong

Brightly

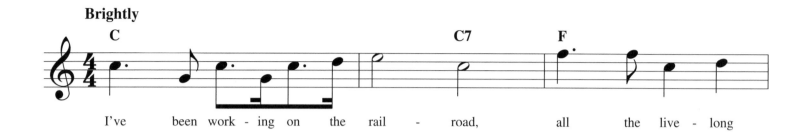

I've been work - ing on the rail - road, all the live - long

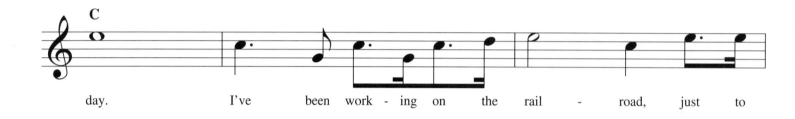

day. I've been work - ing on the rail - road, just to

pass the time a - way. Can't you hear the whis - tle

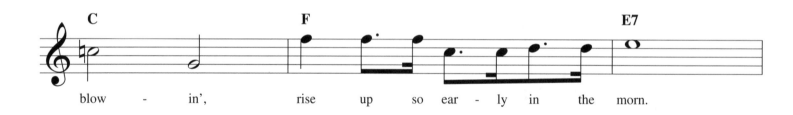

blow - in', rise up so ear - ly in the morn.

Can't you hear the cap - tain shout - in', "Di - nah, blow your horn!"

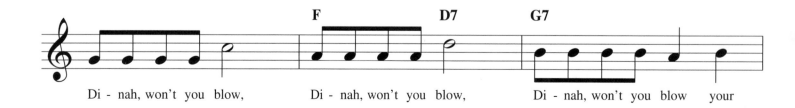

Di - nah, won't you blow, Di - nah, won't you blow, Di - nah, won't you blow your

63

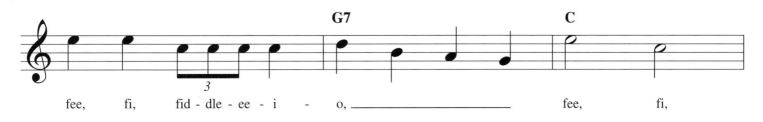

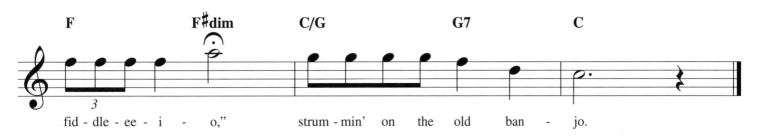

IF YOU'RE HAPPY AND YOU KNOW IT

Words and Music by
L. SMITH

Joyfully

If you're hap - py and you know it,
{ clap your hands.
stamp your foot.
nod your head.
turn a - round.
touch your nose. }
If you're

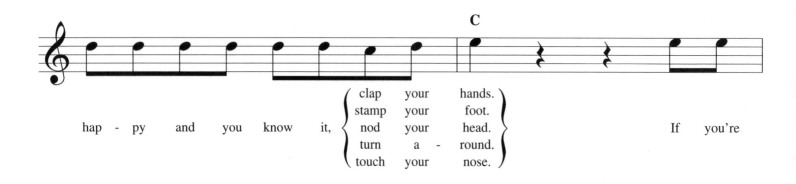

hap - py and you know it,
{ clap your hands.
stamp your foot.
nod your head.
turn a - round.
touch your nose. }
If you're

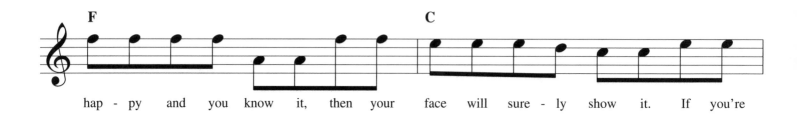

hap - py and you know it, then your face will sure - ly show it. If you're

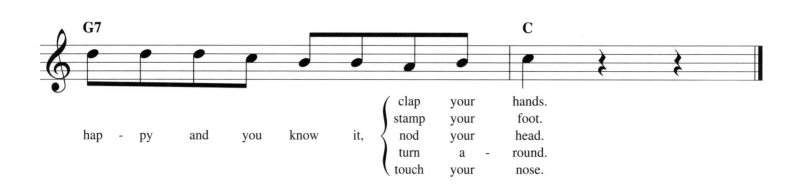

hap - py and you know it,
{ clap your hands.
stamp your foot.
nod your head.
turn a - round.
touch your nose. }

IT'S A SMALL WORLD

from Disneyland Resort® and Magic Kingdom® Park

Words and Music by RICHARD M. SHERMAN
and ROBERT B. SHERMAN

Brightly, in 2

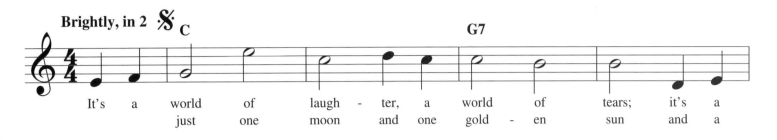

It's a world of laugh - ter, a world of tears; it's a
just one moon and one gold - en sun and a

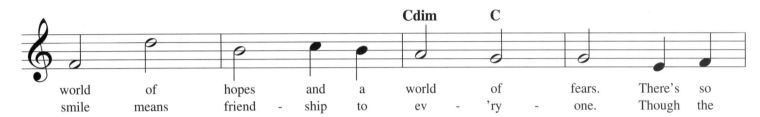

world of hopes and a world of fears. There's so
smile means friend - ship to ev - 'ry - one. Though the

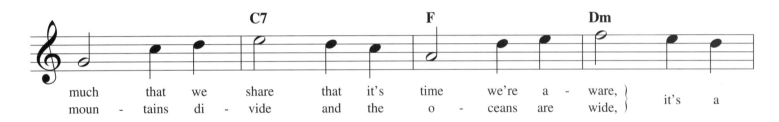

much that we share that it's time we're a - ware,
moun - tains di - vide and the o - ceans are wide, } it's a

small world af - ter all. _____ It's a small world

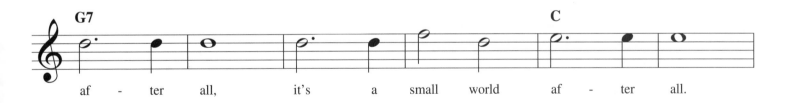

af - ter all, it's a small world af - ter all.

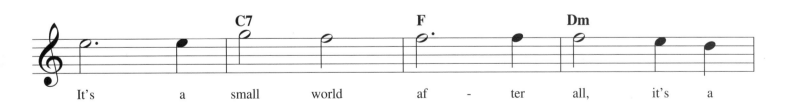

It's a small world af - ter all, it's a

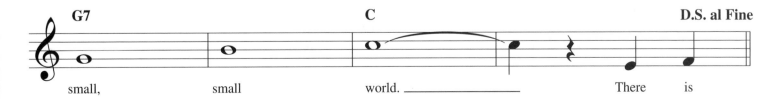

small, small world. _____ There is

IT'S RAINING, IT'S POURING

Traditional

Moderately

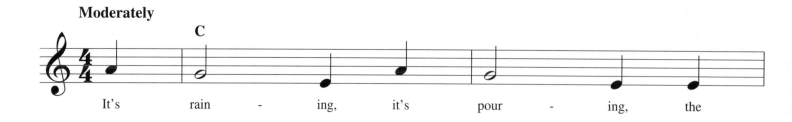

It's rain - ing, it's pour - ing, the

old man is snor - ing. He

went to bed and he bumped his head and he

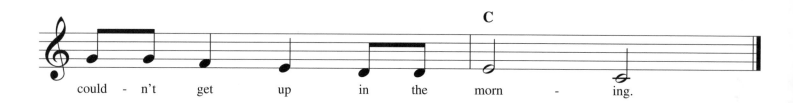

could - n't get up in the morn - ing.

JESUS LOVES ME

Words by ANNA B. WARNER
Music by WILLIAM B. BRADBURY

Moderately

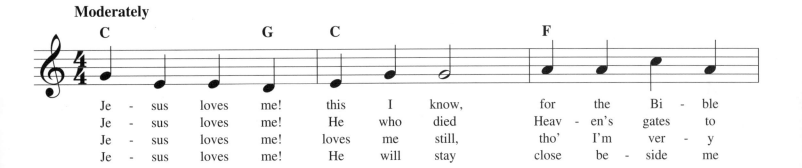

Je - sus loves me! this I know, for the Bi - ble
Je - sus loves me! He who died Heav - en's gates to
Je - sus loves me! loves me still, tho' I'm ver - y
Je - sus loves me! He will stay close be - side me

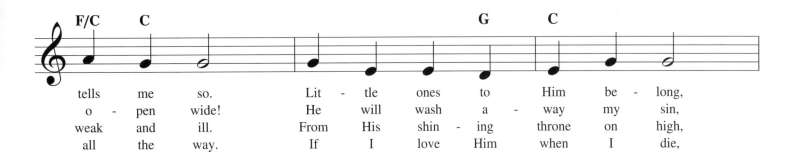

tells me so. Lit - tle ones to Him be - long,
o - pen wide! He will wash a - way my sin,
weak and ill. From His shin - ing throne on high,
all the way. If I love Him when I die,

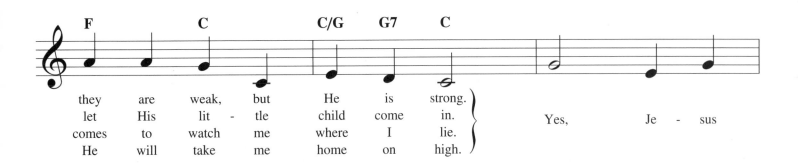

they are weak, but He is strong.
let His lit - tle child come in.
comes to watch me where I lie.
He will take me home on high.
Yes, Je - sus

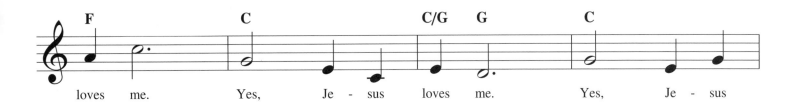

loves me. Yes, Je - sus loves me. Yes, Je - sus

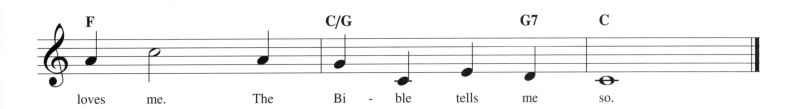

loves me. The Bi - ble tells me so.

JOHN JACOB JINGLEHEIMER SCHMIDT

Traditional

Moderately fast

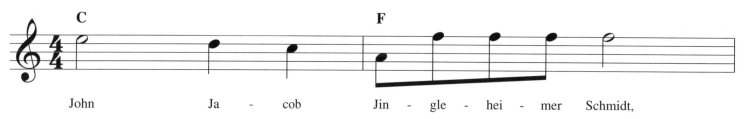

John   Ja - cob   Jin - gle - hei - mer   Schmidt,

His   name   is   my   name,   too.   When -

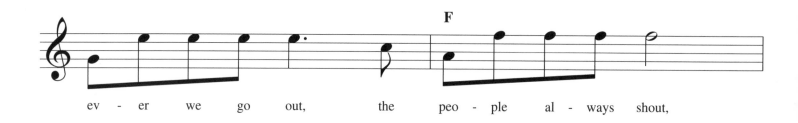

ev - er   we   go   out,   the   peo - ple   al - ways   shout,

"John   Ja - cob   Jin - gle - hei - mer   Schmidt." Dah   dah   dah   dah,   dah   dah   dah.

KUM BA YAH

Traditional Spiritual

Moderately

Kum ba yah, my Lord, Kum ba yah! Kum ba
sing - ing, Lord, Kum ba yah! Some - one's

yah, my Lord, Kum ba yah! Kum ba yah, my Lord, Kum ba
sing - ing, Lord, Kum ba yah! Some - one's sing - ing, Lord, Kum ba

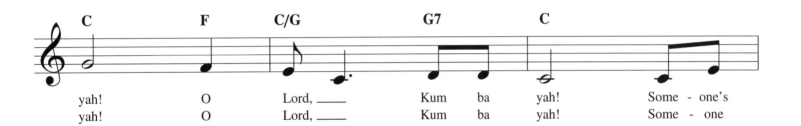

yah! O Lord, ____ Kum ba yah! Some - one's
yah! O Lord, ____ Kum ba yah! Some - one

pray - ing, Lord, Kum ba yah! Some - one's pray - ing, Lord, Kum ba
needs the Lord, Je - sus Christ! Some - one needs the Lord, Je - sus

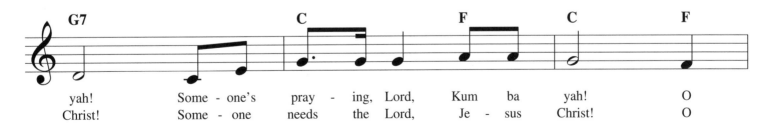

yah! Some - one's pray - ing, Lord, Kum ba yah! O
Christ! Some - one needs the Lord, Je - sus Christ! O

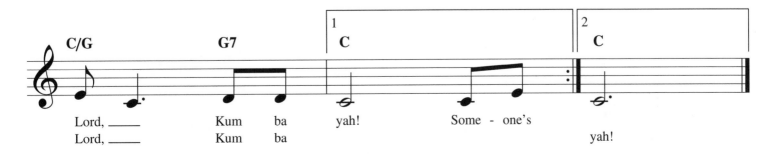

Lord, ____ Kum ba yah! Some - one's
Lord, ____ Kum ba yah! yah!

LAVENDER BLUE
(Dilly Dilly)
from Walt Disney's SO DEAR TO MY HEART

Words by LARRY MOREY
Music by ELIOT DANIEL

Moderately

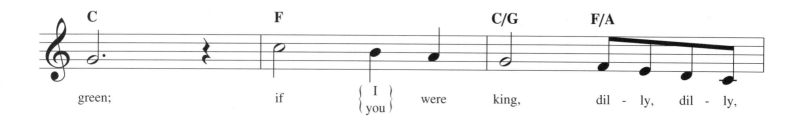

Lav - en - der blue, dil - ly, dil - ly, lav - en - der

green; if {I you} were king, dil - ly, dil - ly,

I'd {you'd} need a queen. Who told me so, dil - ly, dil - ly,

who told me so? I told my - self, dil - ly, dil - ly,

I told me so. If your dil - ly, dil - ly heart feels a

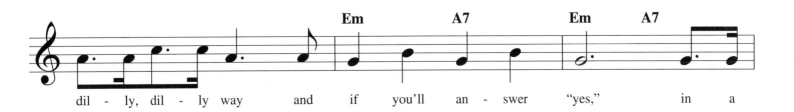

dil - ly, dil - ly way and if you'll an - swer "yes," in a

pret - ty lit - tle church on a dil - ly, dil - ly day { you'll / I'll } be wed in a

dil - ly, dil - ly dress of lav - en - der blue, dil - ly, dil - ly,

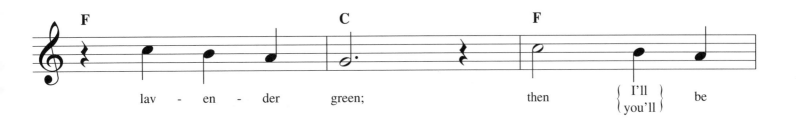

lav - en - der green; then { I'll / you'll } be

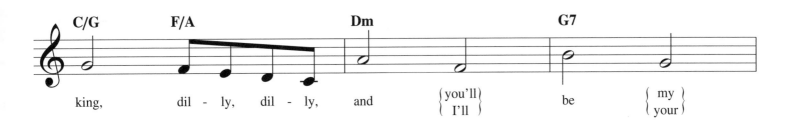

king, dil - ly, dil - ly, and { you'll / I'll } be { my / your }

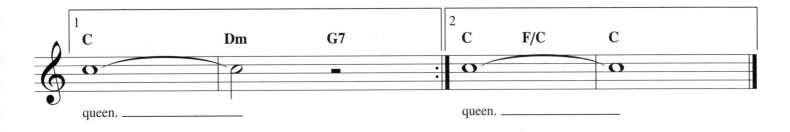

queen. _____   queen. _____

LET'S GO FLY A KITE
from Walt Disney's MARY POPPINS

Words and Music by RICHARD M. SHERMAN
and ROBERT B. SHERMAN

With gusto

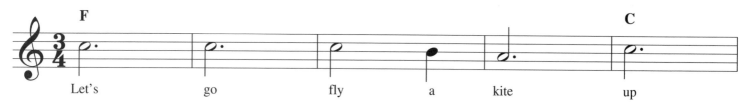

Let's   go   fly   a   kite   up

to   the   high - est   height!   Let's   go

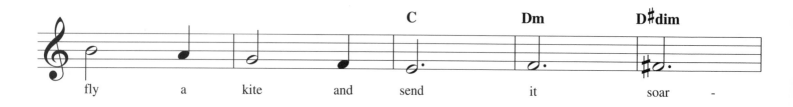

fly   a   kite   and   send   it   soar -

ing   up   through   the   at - mos - phere,

up   where   the   air   is   clear.

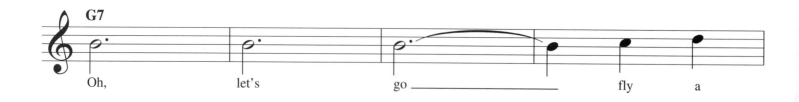

Oh,   let's   go _____   fly   a

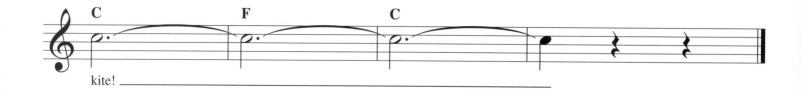

kite! _____

LINUS AND LUCY

By VINCE GUARALDI

THE MARVELOUS TOY

Words and Music by
TOM PAXTON

Moderately

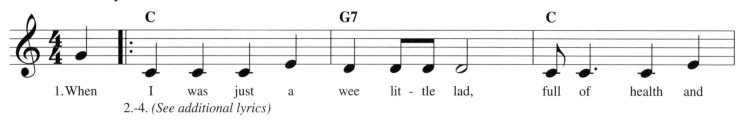

1. When I was just a wee lit-tle lad, full of health and
2.-4. *(See additional lyrics)*

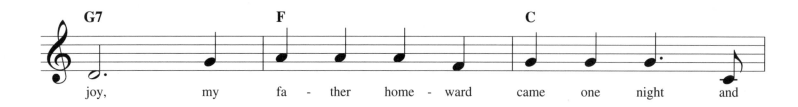

joy, my fa - ther home - ward came one night and

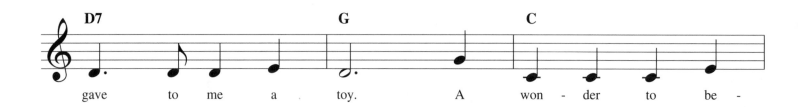

gave to me a toy. A won - der to be -

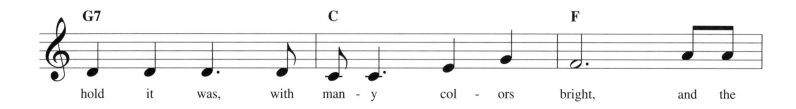

hold it was, with man - y col - ors bright, and the

mo - ment I laid eyes on it, it be - came my heart's de -

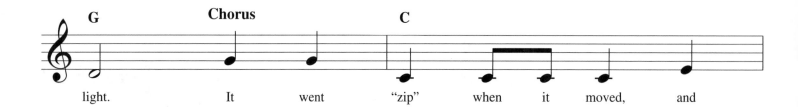

light. It went "zip" when it moved, and

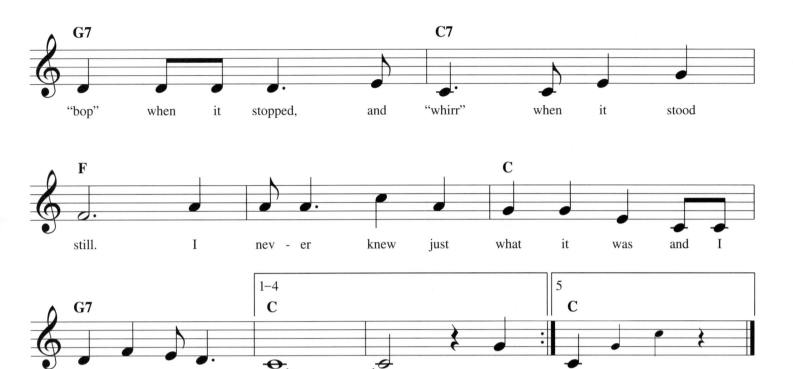

"bop" when it stopped, and "whirr" when it stood still. I nev - er knew just what it was and I guess I nev - er will. _____ The will. *(Instrumental)*

Additional Lyrics

2. The first time that I picked it up, I had a big surprise,
   For right on its bottom were two big buttons that looked like big green eyes.
   I first pushed one and then the other, and then I twisted its lid,
   And when I set it down again, here is what it did:
   Chorus

3. It first marched left and then marched right and then marched under a chair,
   And when I looked where it had gone, it wasn't even there!
   I started to sob and my daddy laughed, for he knew that I would find
   When I turned around my marvelous toy, chugging from behind.
   Chorus

4. Well, the years have gone by too quickly, it seems,
   And I have my own little boy.
   And yesterday I gave to him my marvelous little toy.
   His eyes nearly popped right out of his head, and he gave a squeal of glee.
   Neither one of us knows just what it is, but he loves it, just like me.

   Final Chorus:
   It still goes "zip" when it moves, and "bop" when it stops,
   And "whirr" when it stands still.
   I never knew just what it was
   And I guess I never will.

MARY HAD A LITTLE LAMB

Words by SARAH JOSEPHA HALE
Traditional Music

Brightly

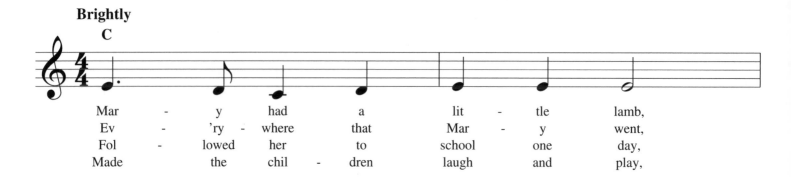

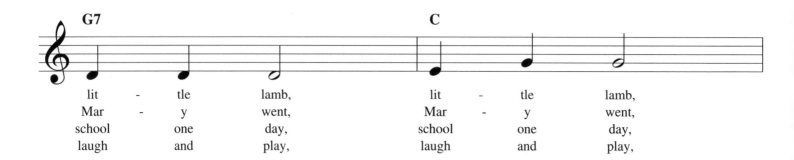

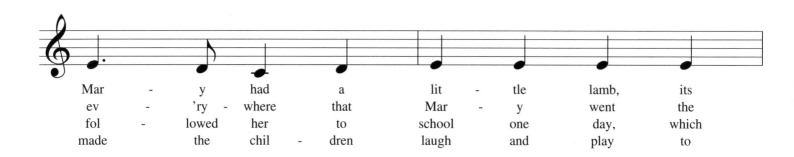

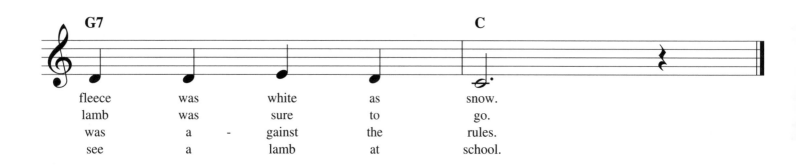

MICHAEL, ROW THE BOAT ASHORE

Traditional Folksong

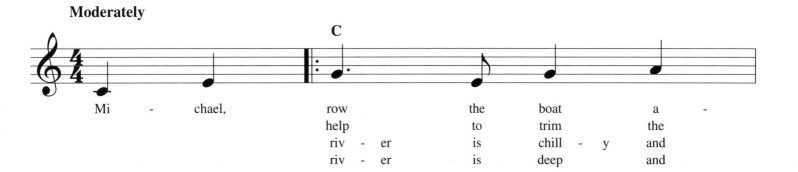

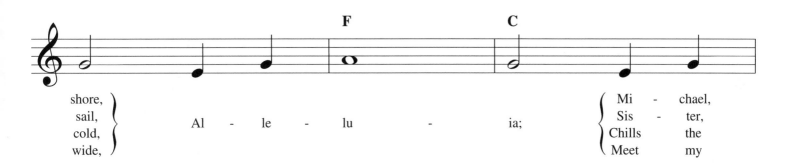

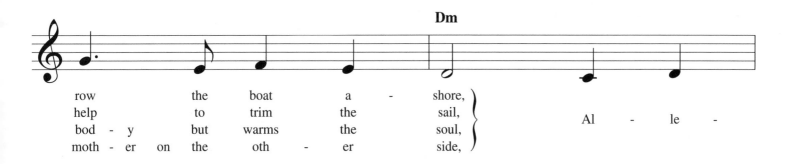

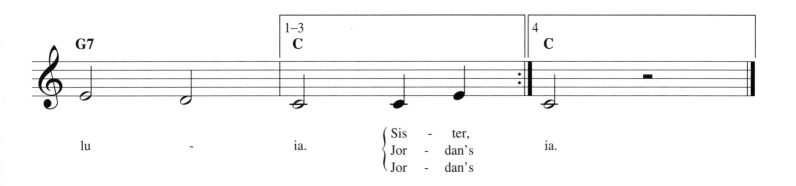

MICKEY MOUSE MARCH
from Walt Disney's THE MICKEY MOUSE CLUB

Words and Music by
JIMMIE DODD

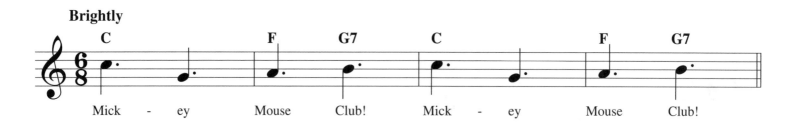

Mick - ey Mouse Club! Mick - ey Mouse Club!

Who's the lead - er of the club that's made for you and me?
Hey, there! Hi, there! Ho, there! You're as wel - come as can be!

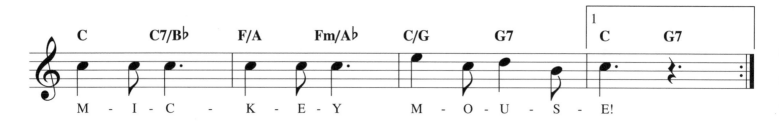

M - I - C - K - E - Y   M - O - U - S - E!

E! Mick - ey Mouse! _____ Mick - ey Mouse! _____

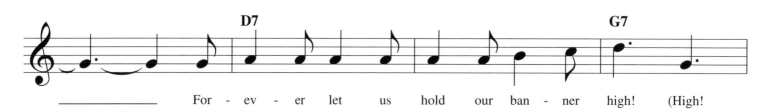

_____ For - ev - er let us hold our ban - ner high! (High!

High! High!) Come a - long and sing a song and join the jam - bo -

ree! M - I - C - K - E - Y   M - O - U - S - E!

THE MUFFIN MAN

Traditional

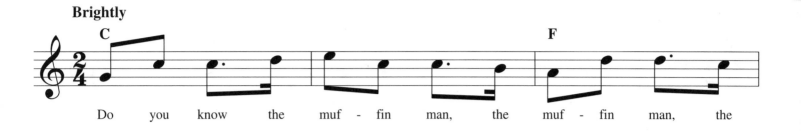

Do you know the muf - fin man, the muf - fin man, the

muf - fin man? Do you know the muf - fin man who

lives in Dru - ry Lane? Yes, we know the muf - fin man, the

muf - fin man, the muf - fin man. Yes, we know the

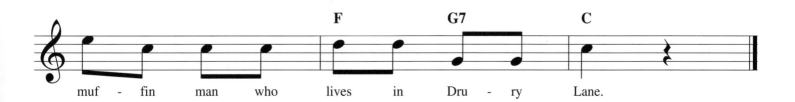

muf - fin man who lives in Dru - ry Lane.

THE MUPPET SHOW THEME
from the Television Series

Words and Music by JIM HENSON
and SAM POTTLE

Bright Rag

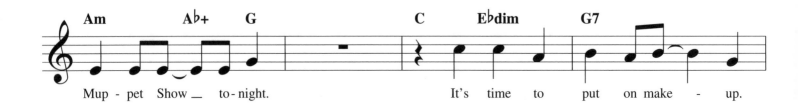

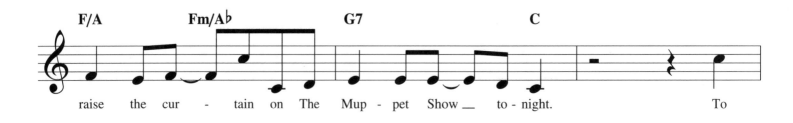

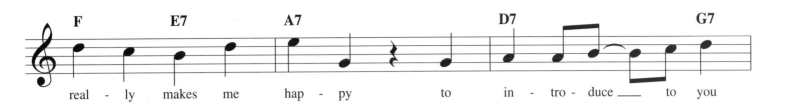

F   E7   A7   D7   G7

real - ly makes me hap - py to in - tro - duce ___ to you

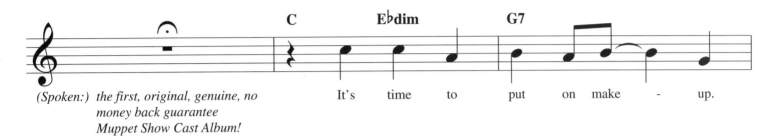

C   E♭dim   G7

(Spoken:) the first, original, genuine, no money back guarantee Muppet Show Cast Album!

It's time to put on make - up.

C   E♭dim   G7   C   C/B♭

It's time to dress up right. ___ It's time to

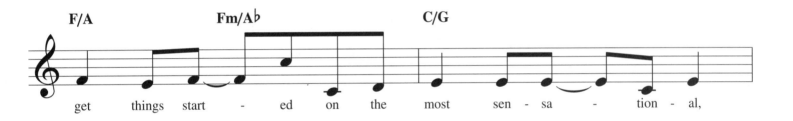

F/A   Fm/A♭   C/G

get things start - ed on the most sen - sa - tion - al,

Am/F♯   F   F/E

in - spi - ra - tion - al, cel - e - bra - tion - al, mup - pet - a - tion - al...

Dm

This is what we call The

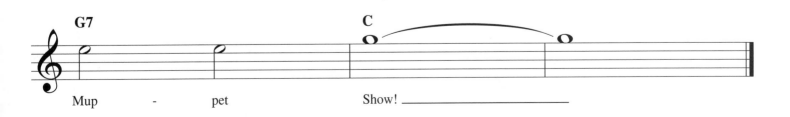

G7   C

Mup - pet Show! ___

MY BONNIE LIES OVER THE OCEAN

Traditional

Moderately

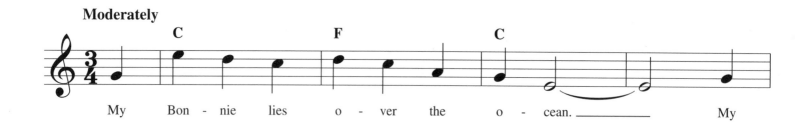

My Bon - nie lies o - ver the o - cean. _____ My

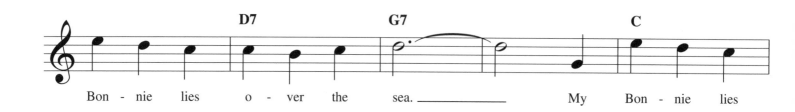

Bon - nie lies o - ver the sea. _____ My Bon - nie lies

o - ver the o - cean. _____ Oh, bring back my Bon - nie to

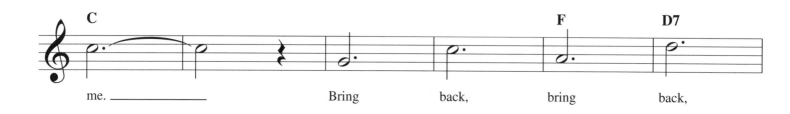

me. _____ Bring back, bring back,

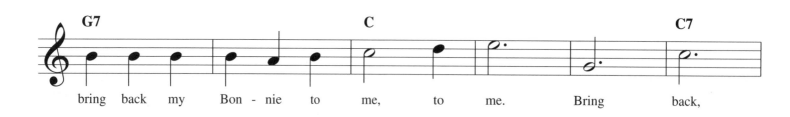

bring back my Bon - nie to me, to me. Bring back,

bring back, oh, bring back my Bon - nie to me. _____

MY COUNTRY, 'TIS OF THEE
(America)

Words by SAMUEL FRANCIS SMITH
Music from *Thesaurus Musicus*

Flowing

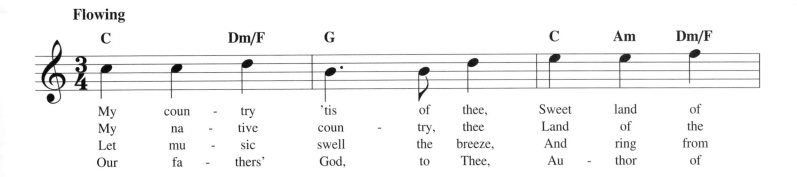

My coun - try 'tis of thee, Sweet land of
My na - tive coun - try, thee Land of the
Let mu - sic swell the breeze, And ring from
Our fa - thers' God, to Thee, Au - thor of

lib - er - ty, Of thee I sing: Land where my
no - ble, free, Thy name I love. I love thy
all the trees Sweet free - dom's song. Let mor - tal
lib - er - ty, To Thee we sing: Long may our

fa - thers died, Land of the pil - grim's pride;
rocks and rills, Thy woods and tem - pled hills;
tongues a - wake, Let all that breathe par - take;
land be bright With free - dom's ho - ly light;

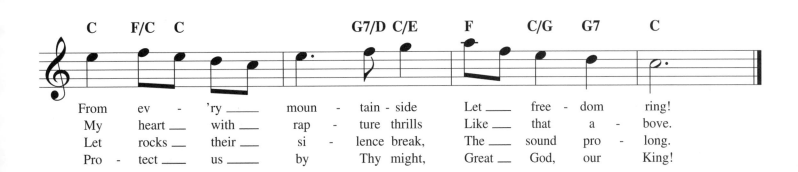

From ev - 'ry ___ moun - tain - side Let ___ free - dom ring!
My heart ___ with ___ rap - ture thrills Like ___ that a - bove.
Let rocks ___ their ___ si - lence break, The ___ sound pro - long.
Pro - tect ___ us ___ by Thy might, Great ___ God, our King!

MY FAVORITE THINGS
from THE SOUND OF MUSIC

Lyrics by OSCAR HAMMERSTEIN II
Music by RICHARD RODGERS

Moderately

Rain - drops on ros - es and whis - kers on kit - tens,
Cream col - ored po - nies and crisp ap - ple strud - els,

bright cop - per ket - tles and warm wool - en mit - tens,
door - bells and sleigh - bells and schnitz - el with noo - dles,

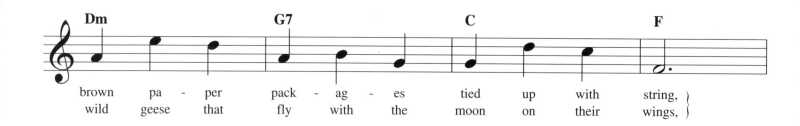

brown pa - per pack - ag - es tied up with string, }
wild geese that fly with the moon on their wings, }

these are a few of my fa - vor - ite things.

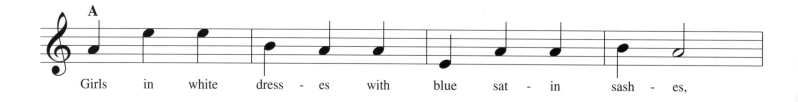

Girls in white dress - es with blue sat - in sash - es,

snow - flakes that stay on my nose and eye - lash - es,

85

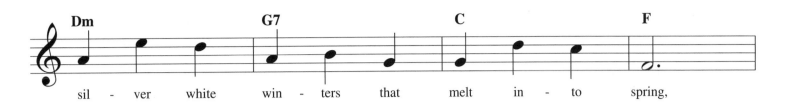

sil - ver white win - ters that melt in - to spring,

these are a few of my fa - vor - ite things.

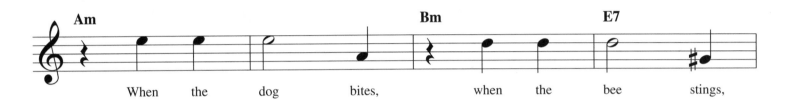

When the dog bites, when the bee stings,

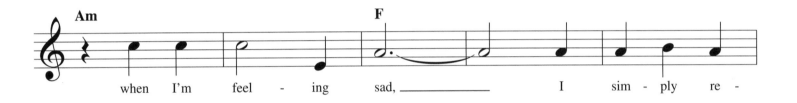

when I'm feel - ing sad, _____ I sim - ply re -

mem - ber my fa - vor - ite things and

then I don't feel so

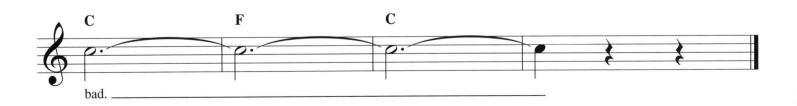

bad. _____

OH! SUSANNA

Words and Music by
STEPHEN C. FOSTER

Lively

1. I ____ come from Al - a - bam - a with a ban - jo on my
   rained all night the day I left, the weath - er it was
2. *(See additional lyrics)*

knee. I'm ____ goin' to Lou' - si - an - a, my Su - san - na for to
dry. The ____ sun so hot I froze to death. Su - san - na, don't you

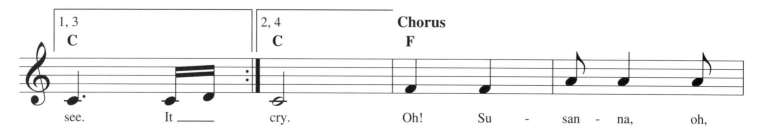

1, 3   **2, 4**   **Chorus**

see. It ____ cry. Oh! Su - san - na, oh,

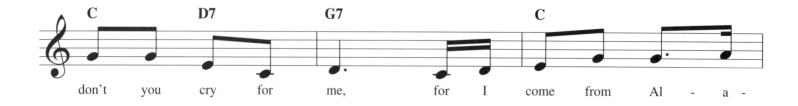

don't you cry for me, for I come from Al - a -

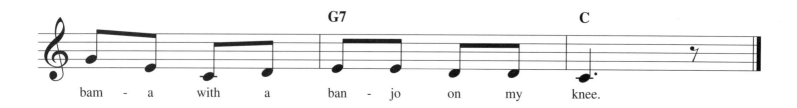

bam - a with a ban - jo on my knee.

Additional Lyrics

2. I had a dream the other night
   When everything was still.
   I thought I saw Susanna
   A-coming down the hill.
   The buckwheat cake was in her mouth,
   The tear was in her eye,
   Say I, "I'm coming from the South.
   Susanna, don't you cry."
   Chorus

OH WHERE, OH WHERE HAS MY LITTLE DOG GONE

Words by Sep. Winner
Traditional Melody

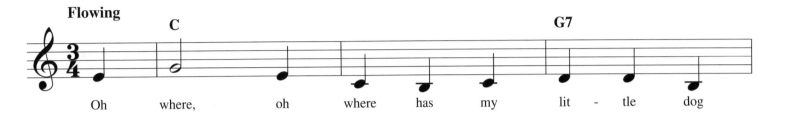

Oh where, oh where has my lit - tle dog

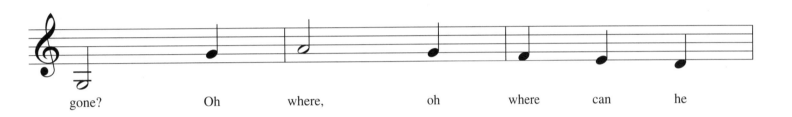

gone? Oh where, oh where can he

be? _____ With his ears cut

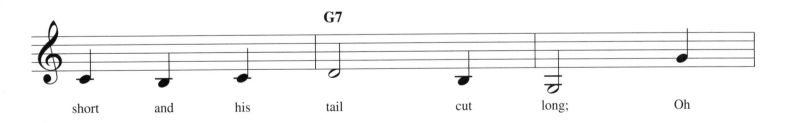

short and his tail cut long; Oh

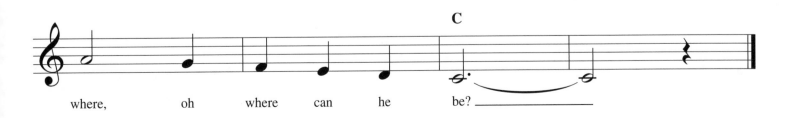

where, oh where can he be? _____

THE OLD GRAY MARE

Words and Music by
J. WARNER

Moderately

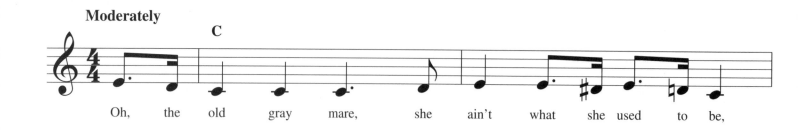

Oh, the old gray mare, she ain't what she used to be,

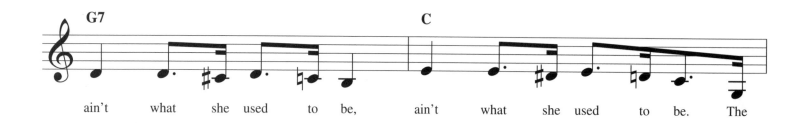

ain't what she used to be, ain't what she used to be. The

old gray mare, she ain't what she used to be man-y long years a-

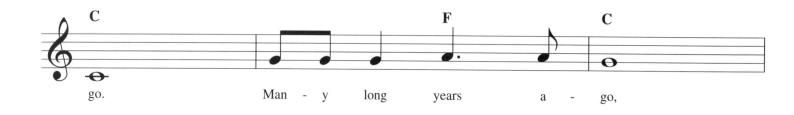

go. Man-y long years a - go,

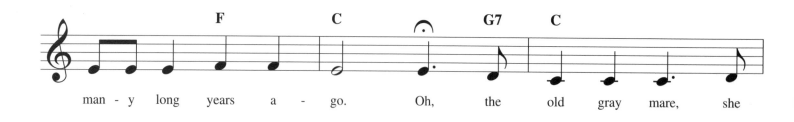

man-y long years a - go. Oh, the old gray mare, she

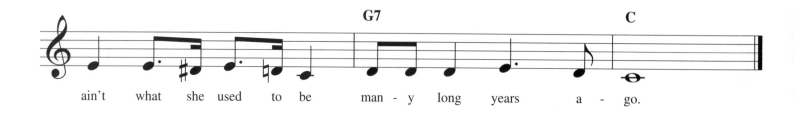

ain't what she used to be man-y long years a - go.

OLD MacDONALD

Traditional Children's Song

Moderately

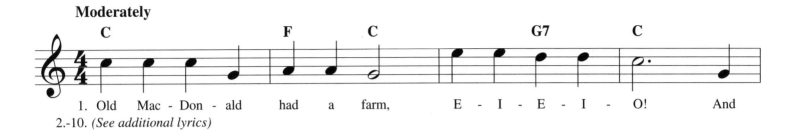

1. Old Mac - Don - ald had a farm, E - I - E - I - O! And
2.-10. *(See additional lyrics)*

on this farm he had a duck, E - I - E - I - O! With a

quack - quack here, and a quack - quack there, here a quack, there a quack,

ev - 'ry - where a quack, quack. Old Mac - Don - ald

had a farm, E - I - E - I - O!

Additional Lyrics

2. Old MacDonald had a farm,
   E-I-E-I-O!
   And on his farm he had a chick,
   E-I-E-I-O!
   With a chick, chick here,
   And a chick, chick there,
   Here a chick, there a chick,
   Everywhere a chick, chick.
   Old MacDonald had a farm,
   E-I-E-I-O!

Other verses:

3. Cow – moo, moo
4. Dog – bow, bow
5. Pig – oink, oink
6. Rooster – cock-a-doodle, cock-a-doodle
7. Turkey – gobble, gobble
8. Cat – meow, meow
9. Horse – neigh, neigh
10. Donkey – hee-haw, hee-haw

ON TOP OF SPAGHETTI

Words and Music by
TOM GLAZER

Moderately fast, with spirit

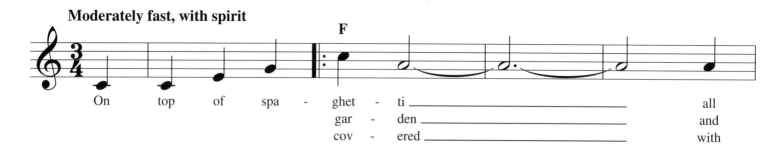

On top of spa - ghet - ti _____ all
gar - den _____ and
cov - ered _____ with

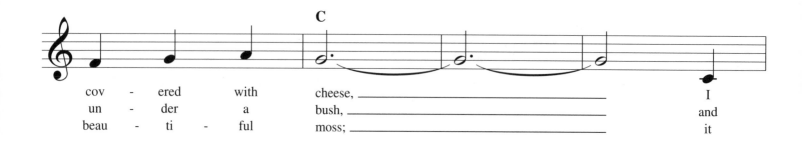

cov - ered with cheese, _____ I
un - der a bush, _____ and
beau - ti - ful moss; _____ it

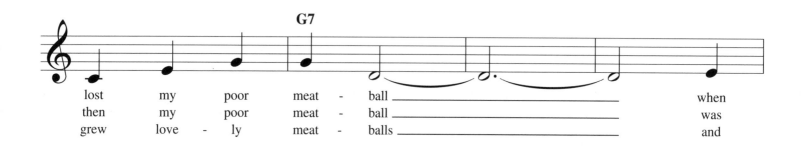

lost my poor meat - ball _____ when
then my poor meat - ball _____ was
grew love - ly meat - balls _____ and

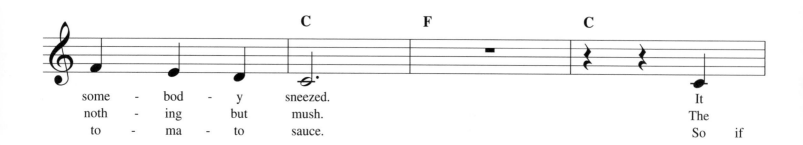

some - bod - y sneezed. It
noth - ing but mush. The
to - ma - to sauce. So if

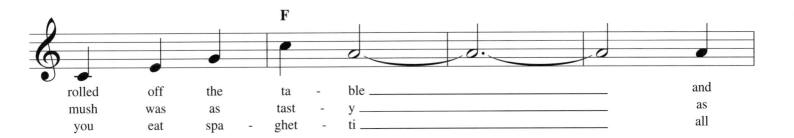

rolled off the ta - ble _____ and
mush was as tast - y _____ as
you eat spa - ghet - ti _____ all

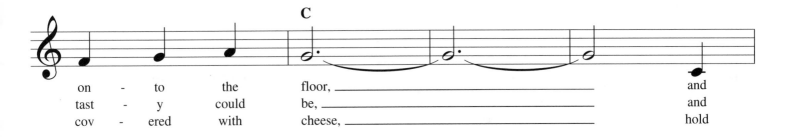

on - to the floor, _____ and
tast - y could be, _____ and
cov - ered with cheese, _____ hold

G7

then my poor meat - ball _____ rolled
ear - ly next sum - mer, _____ it grew
on to your meat - balls _____ and

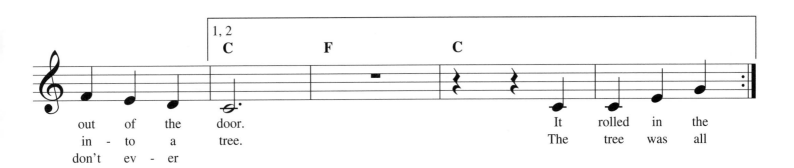

1, 2
C   F   C

out of the door.
in - to a tree.
don't ev - er

It rolled in the
The tree was all

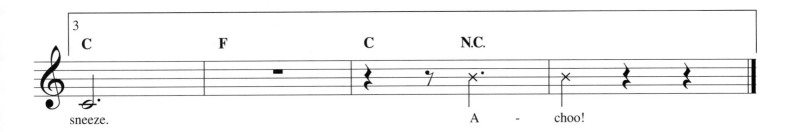

3
C   F   C   N.C.

sneeze.

A - choo!

POP GOES THE WEASEL

Traditional

Moderately

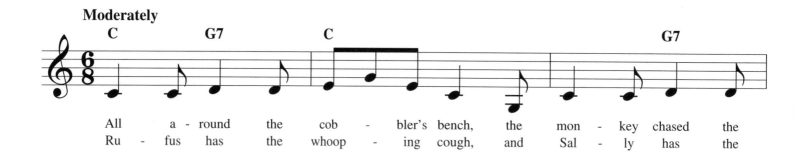

All a - round the cob - bler's bench, the mon - key chased the
Ru - fus has the whoop - ing cough, and Sal - ly has the

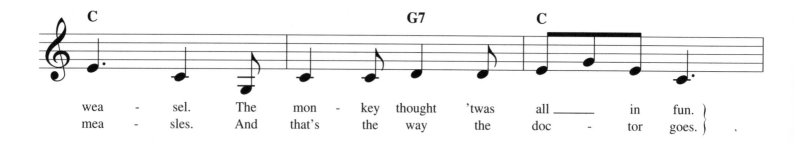

wea - sel. The mon - key thought 'twas all ____ in fun.
mea - sles. And that's the way the doc - tor goes.

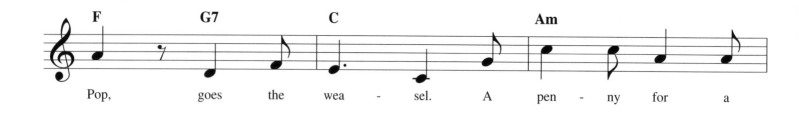

Pop, goes the wea - sel. A pen - ny for a

spool ____ of thread, a pen - ny for ____ a nee - dle.

That's the way the mon - key goes. Pop, goes the wea - sel.

PRAISE HIM, ALL YE LITTLE CHILDREN

Traditional Words
Music by CAREY BONNER

Joyfully

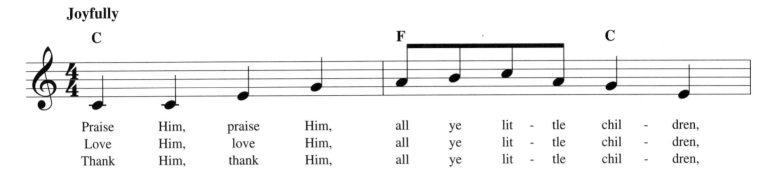

Praise Him, praise Him, all ye lit - tle chil - dren,
Love Him, praise love Him, all ye lit - tle chil - dren,
Thank Him, thank Him, all ye lit - tle chil - dren,

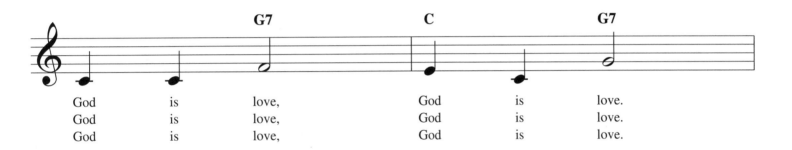

God is love, God is love.
God is love, God is love.
God is love, God is love.

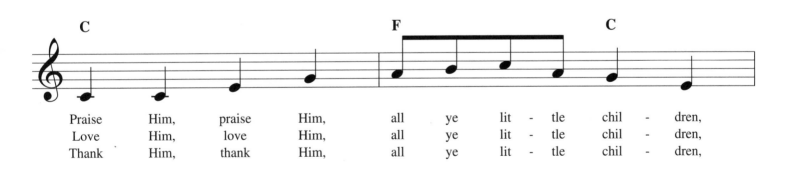

Praise Him, praise Him, all ye lit - tle chil - dren,
Love Him, love Him, all ye lit - tle chil - dren,
Thank Him, thank Him, all ye lit - tle chil - dren,

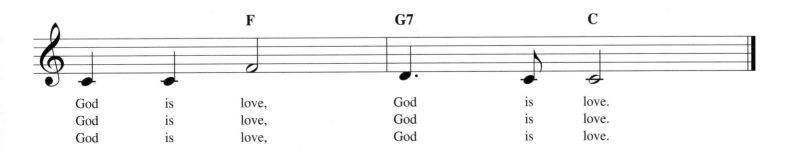

God is love, God is love.
God is love, God is love.
God is love, God is love.

PUFF THE MAGIC DRAGON

Words and Music by LENNY LIPTON
and PETER YARROW

Moderately

1. Puff, the Mag - ic Drag - on, lived by ___ the
2.-4. *(See additional lyrics)*

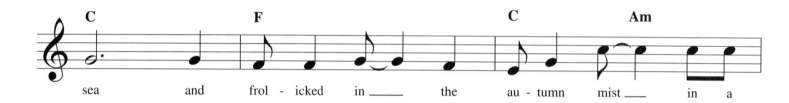

sea and frol - icked in ___ the au - tumn mist ___ in a

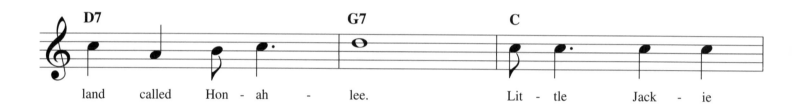

land called Hon - ah - lee. Lit - tle Jack - ie

Pa - per loved that ras - cal Puff, and

brought him strings and seal - ing wax ___ and oth - er fan - cy

Chorus

stuff. Oh! Puff, the Mag - ic Drag - on,

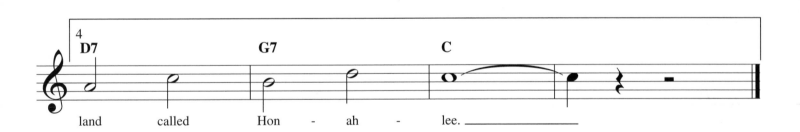

Additional Lyrics

2. Together they would travel on a boat with billowed sail;
   Jackie kept a lookout perched on Puff's gigantic tail.
   Noble kings and princes would bow whene'er they came;
   Pirate ships would low'r their flag when Puff roared out his name. Oh!
   Chorus

3. A dragon lives forever, but not so little boys;
   Painted wings and giant rings make way for other toys.
   One grey night it happened, Jackie Paper came no more.
   And Puff, that magic dragon, he ceased his fearless roar. Oh!
   Chorus

4. His head was bent in sorrow, green scales fell like rain;
   Puff no longer went to play along the cherry lane.
   Without his life-long friend, Puff could not be brave,
   So Puff, that mighty dragon, sadly slipped into his cave. Oh!
   Chorus

THE RAINBOW CONNECTION
from THE MUPPET MOVIE

Words and Music by PAUL WILLIAMS
and KENNETH L. ASCHER

Moderately, with a lilt

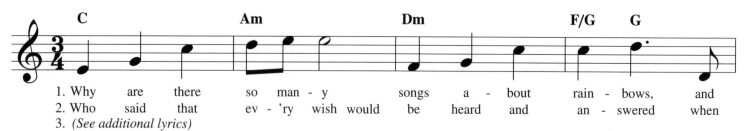

1. Why are there so man-y songs a-bout rain-bows, and
2. Who said that ev-'ry wish would be heard and an-swered when
3. *(See additional lyrics)*

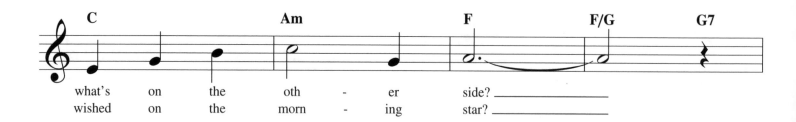

what's on the oth-er side? _____
wished on the morn-ing star? _____

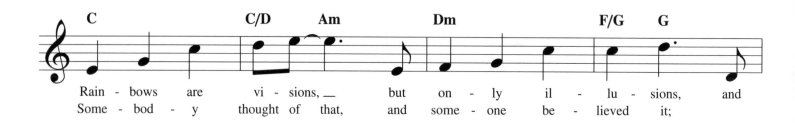

Rain-bows are vi-sions, __ but on-ly il-lu-sions, and
Some-bod-y thought of that, and some-one be-lieved it;

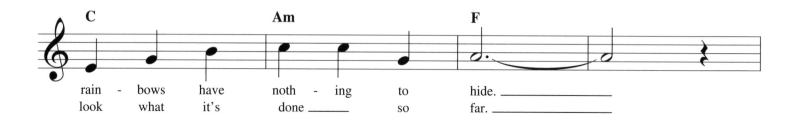

rain-bows have noth-ing to hide. _____
look what it's done _____ so far. _____

So we've been told, and some choose to be-lieve it,
What's so a-maz-ing that keeps us star-gaz-ing, and

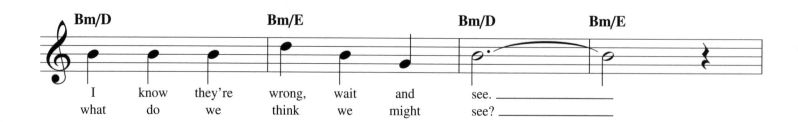

I know they're wrong, wait and see. _____
what do we think we might see? _____

97

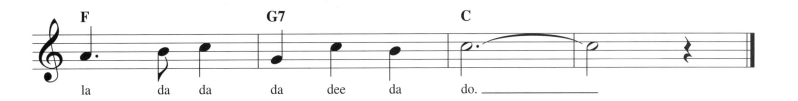

Additional Lyrics

3. Have you been half asleep and have you heard voices?
   I've heard them calling my name.
   Is this the sweet sound that calls the young sailors?
   The voice might be one and the same.
   I've heard it too many times to ignore it.
   It's something that I'm s'posed to be.
   Someday we'll find it,
   The rainbow connection;
   The lovers, the dreamers and me.

RUBBER DUCKIE
from the Television Series SESAME STREET

Words and Music by
JEFF MOSS

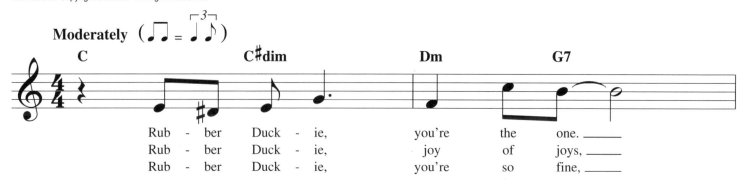

Rub - ber Duck - ie, you're the one. _____
Rub - ber Duck - ie, joy of joys, _____
Rub - ber Duck - ie, you're so fine, _____

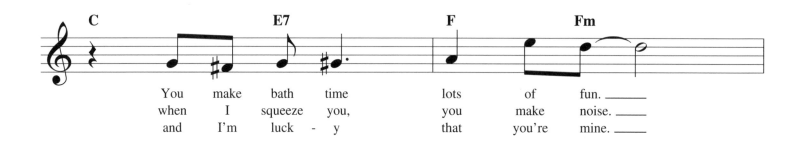

You make bath time lots of fun. _____
when I squeeze you, you make noise. _____
and I'm luck - y that you're mine. _____

Rub - ber Duck - ie, I'm aw - ful - ly fond of
Rub - ber Duck - ie, you're my ver - y best friend it's
Rub - ber Duck - ie, I'm

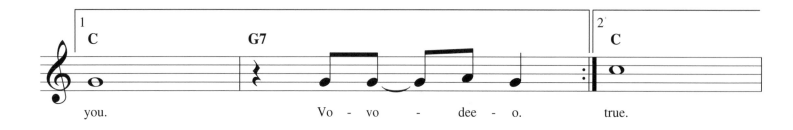

you.
Vo - vo - dee - o. true.

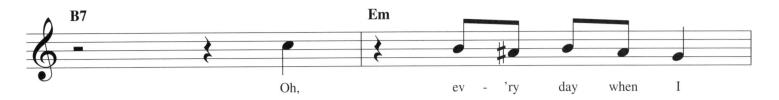

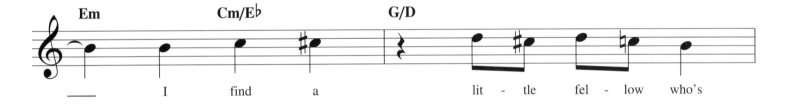

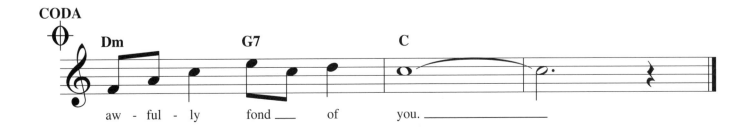

RUMBLY IN MY TUMBLY
from Walt Disney's THE MANY ADVENTURES OF WINNIE THE POOH

Words and Music by RICHARD M. SHERMAN
and ROBERT B. SHERMAN

Easy Latin tempo

Hum - dum dum dum   hum - dee dum dum,   I'm so rum - bly
I don't need a   pot of hon - ey.   I'd be grate - ful

in my tum - bly.   Time to munch an   ear - ly lunch - eon,
for a plate - full.   When I'm rum - bly   in my tum - bly,

time   for some - thing   sweet!   Oh, I would - n't climb this
then   it's time to   eat!   It's the taste - ful thing to

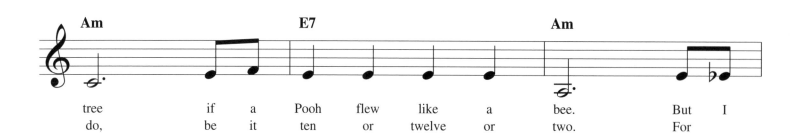

tree   if a Pooh flew like a   bee.   But I
do,   be it ten or twelve or   two.   For

101

would - n't be a bear then, so I guess I would - n't
an - y - time is food time when you set your clock on

care then!
Pooh time!

Bears love hon - ey, and I'm a Pooh bear,

so I do care, so I'll climb there. I'm so rum - bly

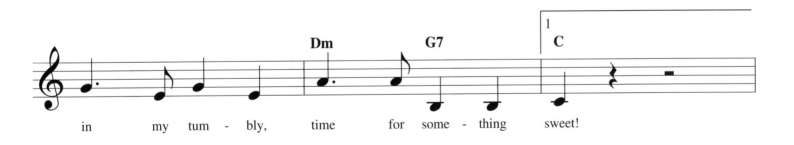

in my tum - bly, time for some - thing sweet!

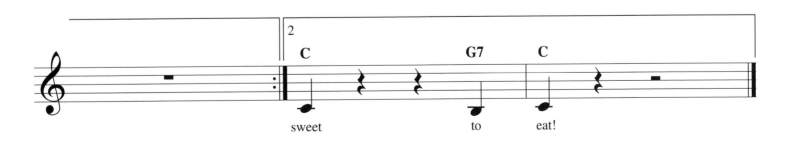

sweet to eat!

SAILING, SAILING

Words and Music by
GODFREY MARKS

Briskly

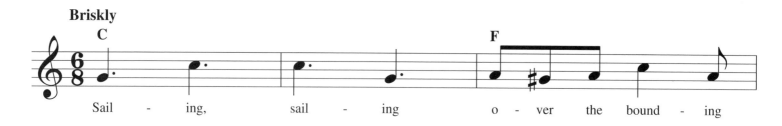

Sail - ing, sail - ing o - ver the bound - ing

main, _____ for man - y a storm - y wind shall blow ere

Jack ___ comes home a - gain! _____ Sail - ing, sail - ing

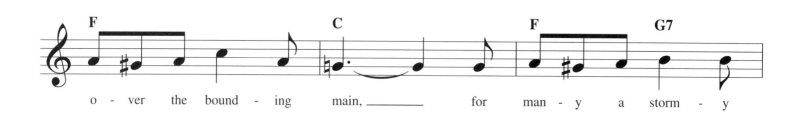

o - ver the bound - ing main, _____ for man - y a storm - y

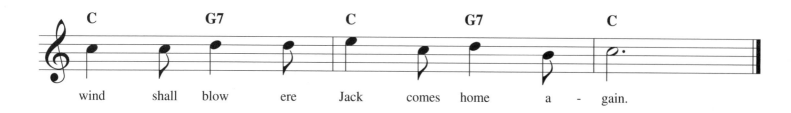

wind shall blow ere Jack comes home a - gain.

SHE'LL BE COMIN' 'ROUND THE MOUNTAIN

Traditional

Rhythmically

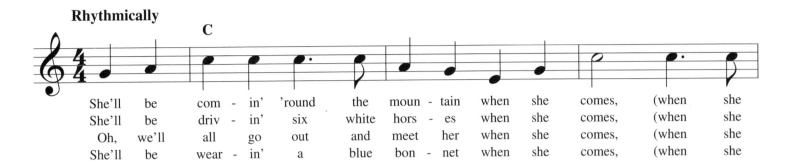

She'll be com - in' 'round the moun - tain when she comes, (when she
She'll be driv - in' six white hors - es when she comes, (when she
Oh, we'll all go out and meet her when she comes, (when she
She'll be wear - in' a blue bon - net when she comes, (when she

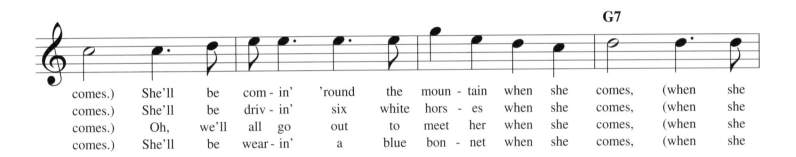

comes.) She'll be com - in' 'round the moun - tain when she comes, (when she
comes.) She'll be driv - in' six white hors - es when she comes, (when she
comes.) Oh, we'll all go out to meet her when she comes, (when she
comes.) She'll be wear - in' a blue bon - net when she comes, (when she

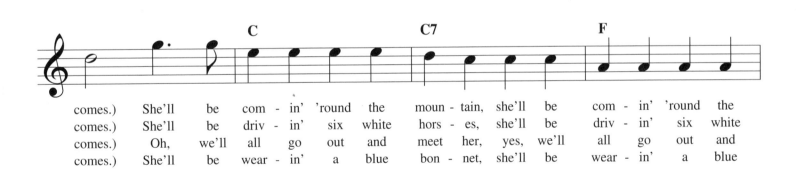

comes.) She'll be com - in' 'round the moun - tain, she'll be com - in' 'round the
comes.) She'll be driv - in' six white hors - es, she'll be driv - in' six white
comes.) Oh, we'll all go out and meet her, yes, we'll all go out and
comes.) She'll be wear - in' a blue bon - net, she'll be wear - in' a blue

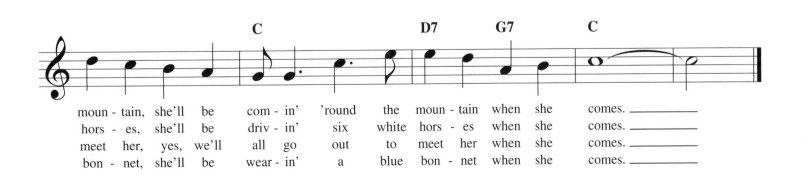

moun - tain, she'll be com - in' 'round the moun - tain when she comes. _____
hors - es, she'll be driv - in' six white hors - es when she comes. _____
meet her, yes, we'll all go out to meet her when she comes. _____
bon - net, she'll be wear - in' a blue bon - net when she comes. _____

SESAME STREET THEME

Words by BRUCE HART,
JON STONE and JOE RAPOSO
Music by JOE RAPOSO

Steady Rock March

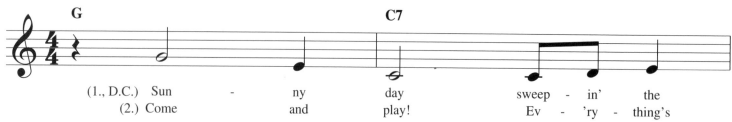

(1., D.C.) Sun - ny day sweep - in' the
(2.) Come and play! Ev - 'ry - thing's

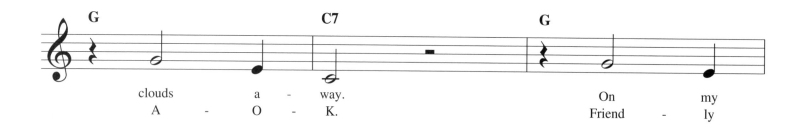

clouds a - way. On my
A - O - K. Friend - ly

way to where the air is sweet. _____
neigh - bors where there, that's where we meet. _____

To Coda

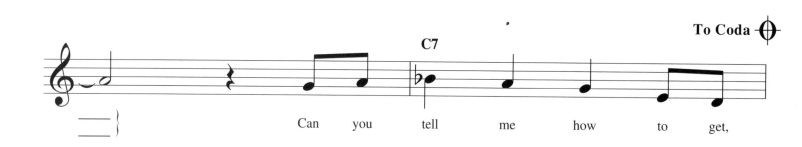

_____ Can you tell me how to get,

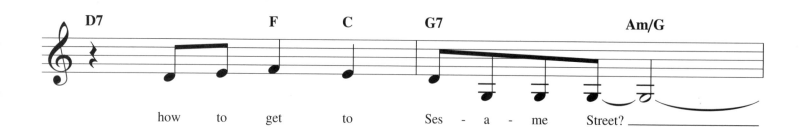

how to get to Ses - a - me Street? _____

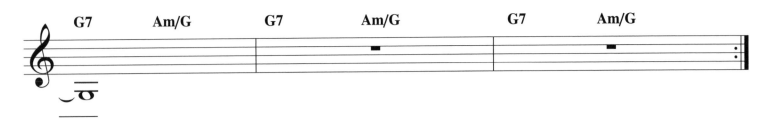

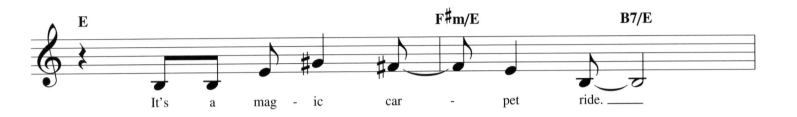

It's a mag - ic car - pet ride. ____

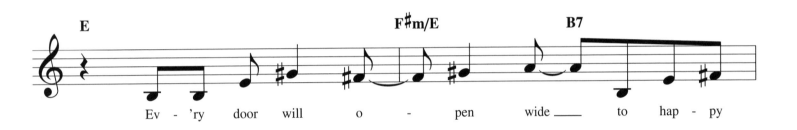

Ev - 'ry door will o - pen wide ____ to hap - py

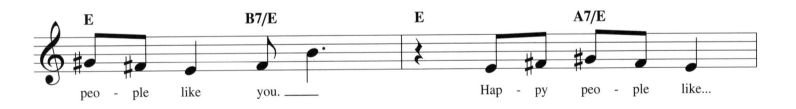

peo - ple like you. ____   Hap - py peo - ple like...

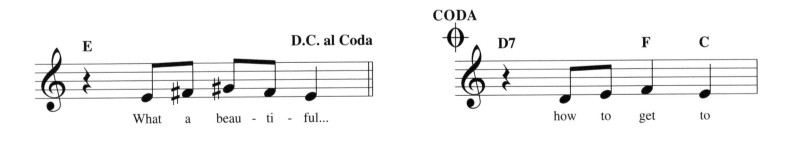

What a beau - ti - ful...   how to get to

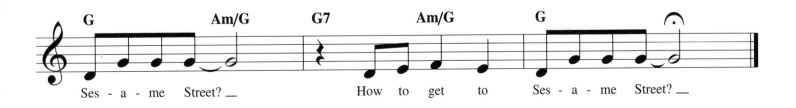

Ses - a - me Street? __   How to get to Ses - a - me Street? __

THE SIAMESE CAT SONG
from Walt Disney's LADY AND THE TRAMP

Words and Music by PEGGY LEE
and SONNY BURKE

Steadily

We are Si - am - ee - iz if you plee - iz, we are Si - am - ee - iz if you

don't please. We are for - mer res - i - dents of Si - am.

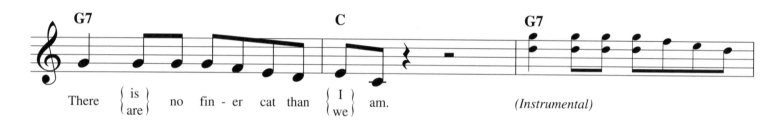

There { is / are } no fin - er cat than { I / we } am. *(Instrumental)*

We are Si - am - ese with ver - y dain - ty claws.

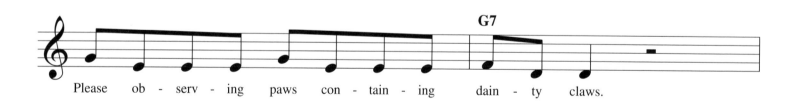

Please ob - serv - ing paws con - tain - ing dain - ty claws.

Now we look - ing o - ver our new dom - i - cile. If we like we stay for may - be

quite a while. *(Instrumental)*

SING
from SESAME STREET

Words and Music by
JOE RAPOSO

Moderately

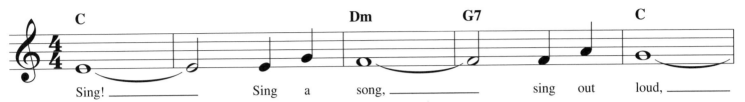

Sing! _____ Sing a song, _____ sing out loud, _____

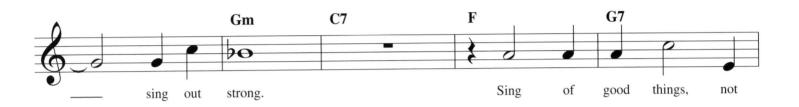

_____ sing out strong. Sing of good things, not

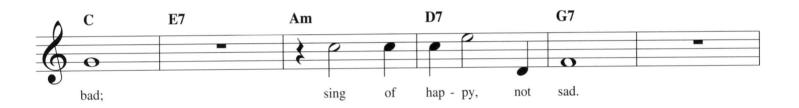

bad; sing of hap - py, not sad.

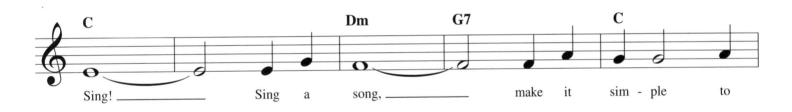

Sing! _____ Sing a song, _____ make it sim - ple to

last your whole life long. _____ Don't wor - ry that it's not good e - nough for

an - y - one else to hear. Sing! _____ Sing a song. _____

La la do la da, la da la do la da, la da da la do la da.   da.

SKIP TO MY LOU

Traditional

Joyfully

Skip,   skip,   skip   to   my   Lou.   Skip,   skip,   skip   to   my   Lou.

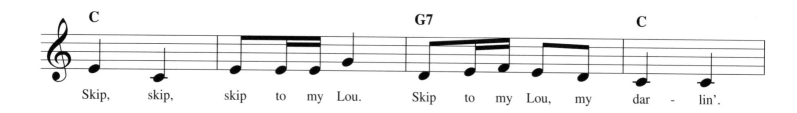

Skip,   skip,   skip   to   my   Lou.   Skip   to   my   Lou,   my   dar - lin'.

Flies	in	the	but - ter - milk,	shoo,	shoo,	shoo!	Flies	in	the	but - ter - milk,
Lost	my		part - ner,	what'll	I	do?	Lost	my		part - ner,
I'll	get	an - oth - er	one,	purtier	than	you.	I'll	get	an - oth - er	one,
Can't	get	a red bird, a		blue - bird - 'll	do.		Can't	get	a red bird, a	

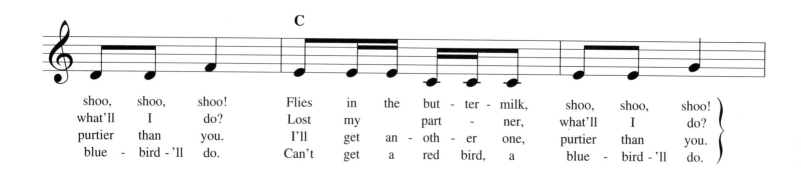

shoo,	shoo,	shoo!	Flies	in	the	but - ter - milk,	shoo,	shoo,	shoo!
what'll	I	do?	Lost	my		part - ner,	what'll	I	do?
purtier	than	you.	I'll	get	an - oth - er	one,	purtier	than	you.
blue - bird - 'll	do.		Can't	get	a red bird, a		blue - bird - 'll	do.

Skip   to   my   Lou,   my   dar - lin'.

SPONGEBOB SQUAREPANTS THEME SONG

from SPONGEBOB SQUAREPANTS

Words and Music by MARK HARRISON, BLAISE SMITH,
STEVE HILLENBURG and DEREK DRYMON

Moderately

Oh! _____ Who lives in a pine-ap-ple un-der the sea?

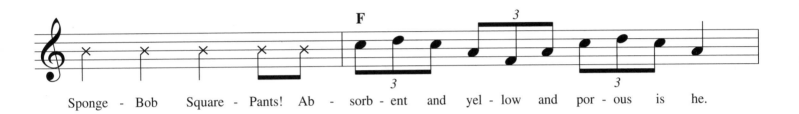

Sponge - Bob Square - Pants! Ab - sorb-ent and yel - low and por - ous is he.

Sponge - Bob Square - Pants! If nau - ti - cal non - sense be some - thing you wish,

Sponge - Bob Square - Pants! then drop on the deck and flop like a fish! Sponge - Bob Square - Pants!

Sponge - Bob Square - Pants! Sponge - Bob Square - Pants! Sponge - Bob Square - Pants! Sponge - Bob Square-

Pants!   (Instrumental)

SO LONG, FAREWELL
from THE SOUND OF MUSIC

Lyrics by OSCAR HAMMERSTEIN II
Music by RICHARD RODGERS

Moderately

So long, fare - well, { Auf wie - der - sehn, good - night, ___ I
Auf wie - der - sehn, a - dieu, ___ a -
Au' voir, auf wie - der - sehn, ___ I'd

hate to go and leave this pret - ty sight. ___ }
dieu, a - dieu, to yieu and yieu and yieu. ___
like to stay and taste my first cham - pagne. ___

(Instrumental)

1, 2   3

So   So long, fare -

well, Auf wie - der - sehn, good - bye, ___ I leave and

heave a sigh and say good - bye. ___ Good - bye. ___

Slower

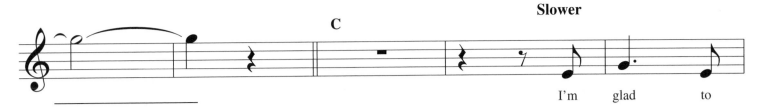

I'm glad to

go, I can - not tell a lie, _____ I flit, I

float, I fleet - ly flee, I fly. _____ *(Instrumental)*

The

sun has gone to bed and so must I. _____ So long, fare -

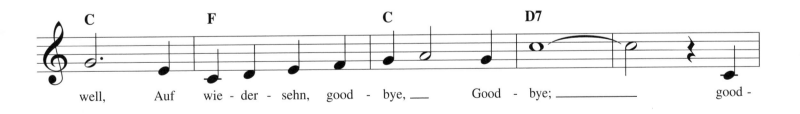

well, Auf wie - der - sehn, good - bye, ___ Good - bye; _____ good -

bye, _____ good - bye, _____ good - bye! _____

SPLISH SPLASH

Words and Music by BOBBY DARIN
and MURRAY KAUFMAN

Moderately fast

Splish splash, I was tak-in' a bath
Bing bang, I saw the whole gang

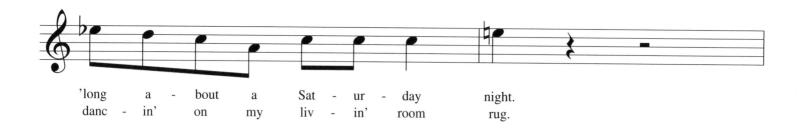

'long a-bout a Sat-ur-day night.
danc-in' on my liv-in' room rug.

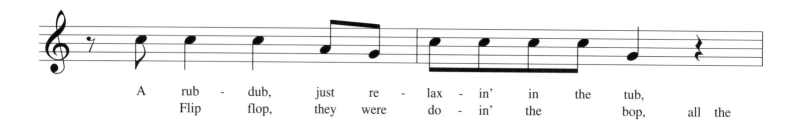

A rub dub, just re-lax-in' in the tub,
Flip flop, just they were do-in' the bop, all the

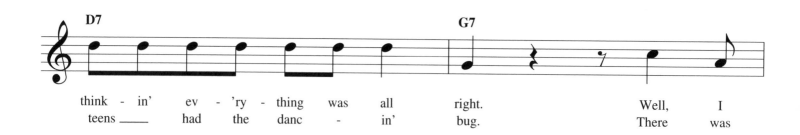

think-in' ev-'ry-thing was all right. Well, I
teens had the danc-in' bug. There was

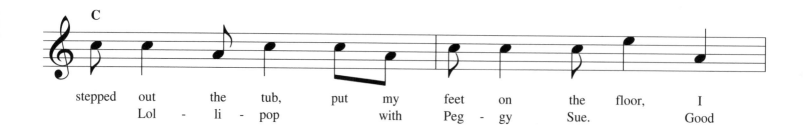

stepped out the tub, put my feet on the floor, I
Lol-li-pop with Peg-gy Sue. Good

A SPOONFUL OF SUGAR
from Walt Disney's MARY POPPINS

Words and Music by RICHARD M. SHERMAN
and ROBERT B. SHERMAN

Fast

C

In ev-'ry job that must be done there is an el-e-ment of fun; you
feath-er-ing his nest has ver-y lit-tle time to rest while
bees that fetch the nec-tar from the flow-ers to the comb nev-er

Ebdim   G7   F

find the fun and snap! the job's a game; ____ and ev-'ry task you un-der-
gath-er-ing his bits of twine and twig. ____ Though quite in-tent in his pur-
tire of ev-er buzz-ing to and fro. ____ Be-cause they take a lit-tle

Ab7   C   D7   G7

take be-comes a piece of cake, a lark! A spree! It's
suit he has a mer-ry tune to toot; he knows a song will
nip from ev-'ry flow-er that they sip, and hence, they find their

G7   C

ver-y clear to see that
move the job a-long. For a spoon-ful of sug-ar helps the med-i-cine go
task is not a grind. For

G7   C   Ebdim

down, the med-i-cine go down, ___ med-i-cine go down. Just a

G7   C

spoon-ful of sug-ar helps the med-i-cine go down in a most de-

G7   C   G7   C

1, 2   3

light-ful way.   A rob-in   way. ____
              The hon-ey

TAKE ME OUT TO THE BALL GAME

Words by JACK NORWORTH
Music by ALBERT VON TILZER

SUPERCALIFRAGILISTICEXPIALIDOCIOUS
from Walt Disney's MARY POPPINS

Words and Music by RICHARD M. SHERMAN
and ROBERT B. SHERMAN

Brightly

Su - per - cal - i - frag - il - is - tic - ex - pi - al - i - do - cious!

E - ven though the sound of it is some - thing quite a - tro - cious.

If you say it loud e - nough, you'll al - ways sound pre - co - cious.

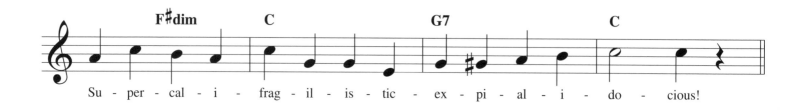

Su - per - cal - i - frag - il - is - tic - ex - pi - al - i - do - cious!

Um did - dle did - dle did - dle, um did - dle ay! Um did - dle did - dle did - dle, um did - dle ay!
{ Be-
  He
  So

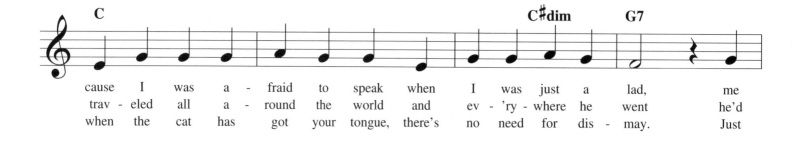

cause I was a - fraid to speak when I was just a lad, me
trav - eled all a - round the world and ev - 'ry - where he went he'd
when the cat has got your tongue, there's no need for dis - may. Just

117

THERE'S A HOLE IN THE BUCKET

Traditional

Moderately

1. There's a hole in the buck - et, dear
2. Well, then fix it, dear Hen - ry, dear
3. With ___ what shall I fix it, dear
4. With a straw, ___ dear Hen - ry, dear
5. But the straw is too long, ___ dear
6. Then ___ cut it, dear Hen - ry, dear

7.-19. *(See additional lyrics)*

Li - za, dear Li - za. There's a hole in the
Hen - ry, dear Hen - ry. Well, ___ fix it, dear
Li - za, dear Li - za? With ___ what shall I
Hen - ry, dear Hen - ry. With a straw, ___ dear
Li - za, dear Li - za. but the straw is too
Hen - ry, dear Hen - ry. Then ___ cut it, dear

buck - et, dear Li - za, a hole!
Hen - ry, dear Hen - ry, fix it!
fix it, dear Li - za, with what?
Hen - ry, dear Hen - ry, a straw.
long, ___ dear Li - za, too long.
Hen - ry, dear Hen - ry, cut it.

Additional Lyrics

7. With what shall I cut it, dear Liza, etc.
8. With a knife, dear Henry, etc.
9. But the knife is too dull, dear Liza, etc.
10. Then sharpen it, dear Henry, etc.
11. With what shall I sharpen it, dear Liza, etc.
12. With a stone, dear Henry, etc.
13. But the stone is too dry, dear Liza, etc.
14. Then wet it, dear Henry, etc.
15. With what shall I wet it, dear Liza, etc.
16. With water, dear Henry, etc.
17. In what shall I carry it, dear Liza, etc.
18. In a bucket, dear Henry, etc.
19. There's a hole in my bucket, dear Liza, etc.

THIS OLD MAN

Traditional

Moderately

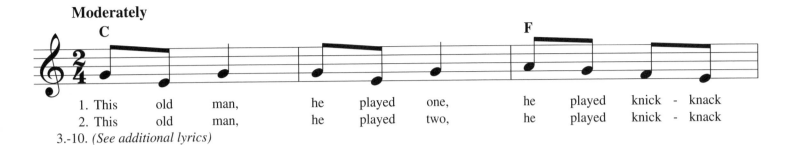

1. This old man, he played one, he played knick - knack
2. This old man, he played two, he played knick - knack

3.-10. *(See additional lyrics)*

Chorus

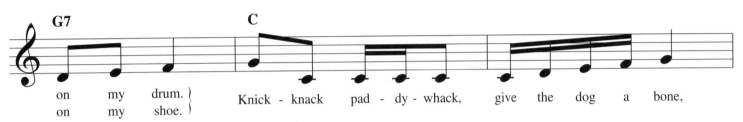

on my drum. }
on my shoe. }
Knick - knack pad - dy - whack, give the dog a bone,

this old man came roll - ing home.

Additional Lyrics

3. This old man, he played three,
   He played knick-knack on my knee.*(Chorus)*

4. This old man, he played four,
   He played knick-knack on my door.*(Chorus)*

5. This old man, he played five,
   He played knick-knack on my hive.*(Chorus)*

6. This old man, he played six,
   He played knick-knack on my sticks.*(Chorus)*

7. This old man, he played seven,
   He played knick-knack up to heaven.*(Chorus)*

8. This old man, he played eight,
   He played knick-knack on the gate. *(Chorus)*

9. This old man, he played nine,
   He played knick-knack on my line.*(Chorus)*

10. This old man, he played ten,
    He played knick-knack over again.*(Chorus)*

THIS LAND IS YOUR LAND

Words and Music by
WOODY GUTHRIE

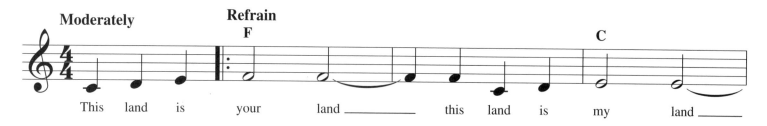

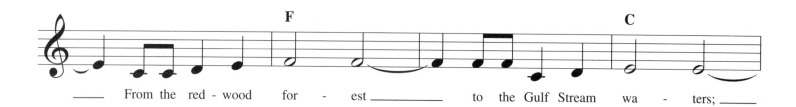

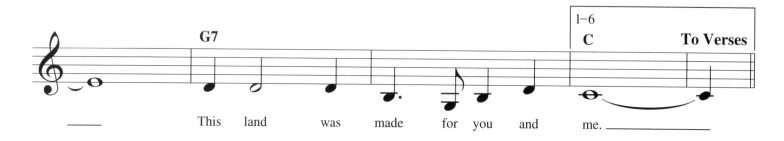

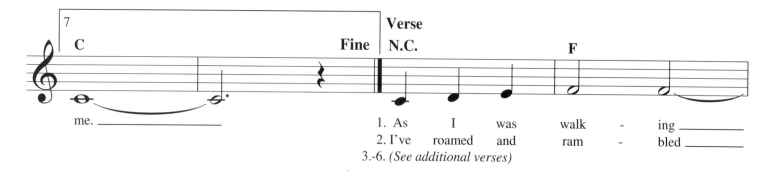

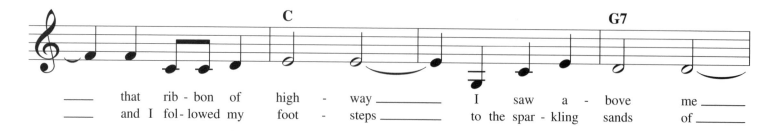

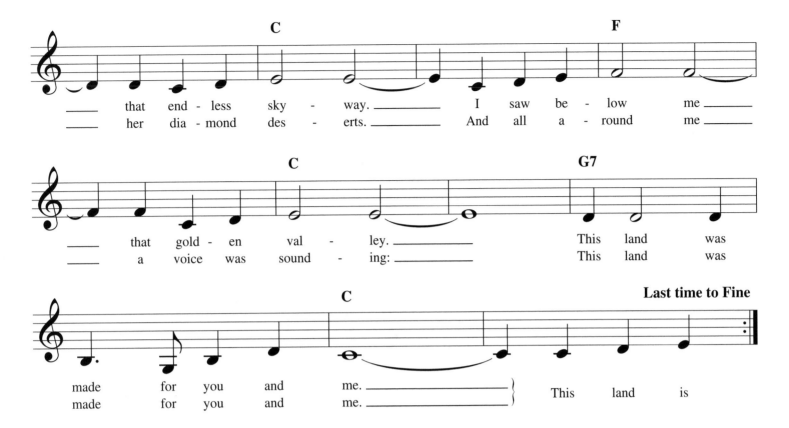

_____	that	end - less	sky -	way. _____	I saw be - low me _____
_____	her	dia - mond	des -	erts. _____	And all a - round me _____

_____	that	gold - en	val - ley. _____	This land was
_____	a	voice was	sound - ing: _____	This land was

Last time to Fine

made	for	you	and	me. _____ }	This land is
made	for	you	and	me. _____ }	

Additional Verses

3. When the sun came shining, and I was strolling,
   And the wheat fields waving, and the dust clouds rolling,
   As the fog was lifting, a voice was chanting:
   This land was made for you and me.
   Refrain

4. As I went walking, I saw a sign there,
   And on the sign it said, "No Trespassing,"
   But on the other side it didn't say nothing;
   That side was made for you and me.
   Refrain

5. In the shadow of the steeple, I saw my people.
   By the relief office, I saw my people.
   As they stood there hungry, I stood there asking:
   Is this land made for you and me?
   Refrain

6. Nobody living can ever stop me
   As I go walking that freedom highway.
   Nobody living can ever make me turn back;
   This land was made for you and me.
   Refrain

THIS TRAIN

Traditional

Moderately

This train is bound for glo - ry, this train, _____
This train don't car - ry no gam - blers, this train, _____
This train is built for speed, now, this train, _____
This train don't car - ry no li - ars, this train, _____
This train don't car - ry no rus - tlers, this train, _____

This train is bound for glo - ry, this train, _____
This train don't car - ry no gam - blers, this train, _____
This train is built for speed, now, this train, _____
This train don't car - ry no li - ars, this train, _____
This train don't car - ry no rus - tlers, this train, _____

This train is bound for glo - ry,
This train don't car - ry no gam - blers,
This train is built for speed now,
This train don't car - ry no li - ars,
This train don't car - ry no rus - tlers,

don't car - ry noth - in' but the right - eous and the ho - ly,
no crap - shoot - ers or _____ mid - night _____ ram - blers,
Fast - est _____ train _____ you _____ ev - er did _____ see, _____
No hyp - o - crites _____ and _____ no _____ high _____ fly - ers,
Side - street _____ walk - ers, _____ two - bit _____ hus - tlers,

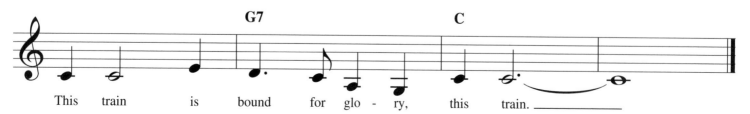

This train is bound for glo - ry, this train. _____

THREE BLIND MICE

Traditional

Briskly

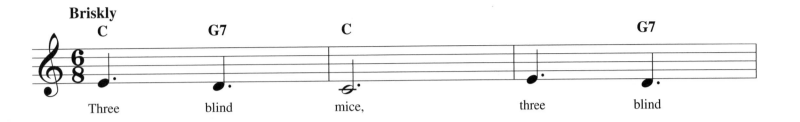

Three   blind   mice,   three   blind

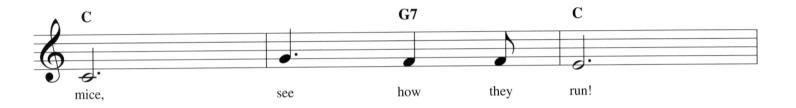

mice,   see   how   they   run!

See   how   they   run! _____   They   all   ran af - ter   the

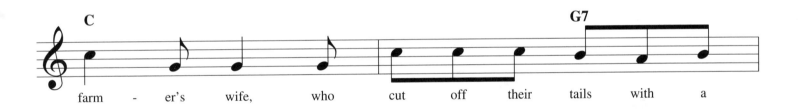

farm - er's   wife,   who   cut   off   their   tails   with   a

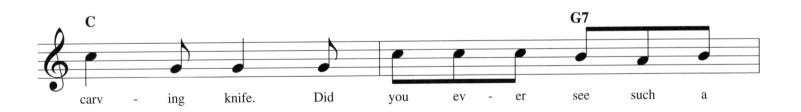

carv - ing   knife.   Did   you   ev - er   see   such   a

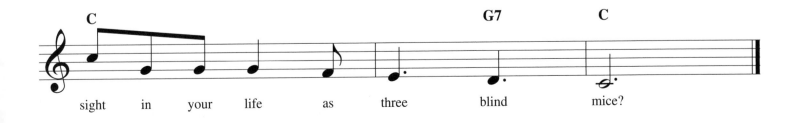

sight   in   your   life   as   three   blind   mice?

TOMORROW
from the Musical Production ANNIE

Lyric by MARTIN CHARNIN
Music by CHARLES STROUSE

Moderately slow

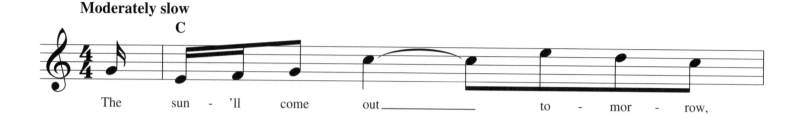

The sun - 'll come out _____ to - mor - row,

bet your bot - tom dol - lar that to - mor-row _____ there'll be

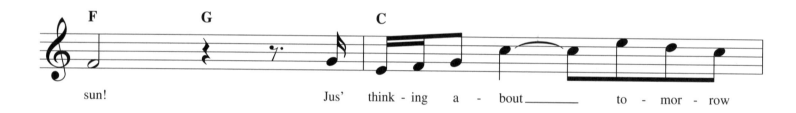

sun! Jus' think - ing a - bout _____ to - mor - row

clears a - way the cob - webs and the sor - row ____ till there's

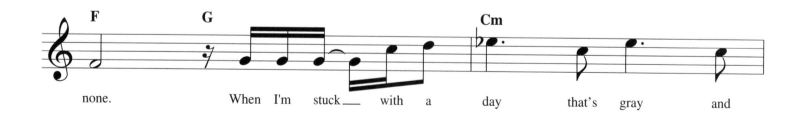

none. When I'm stuck ____ with a day that's gray and

lone - ly, I just stick _____ out my

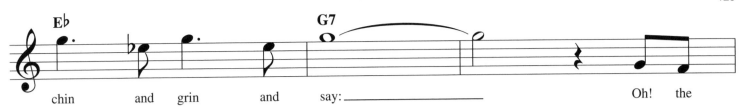

chin and grin and say:_____ Oh! the

sun - 'll come out_____ to - mor - row,

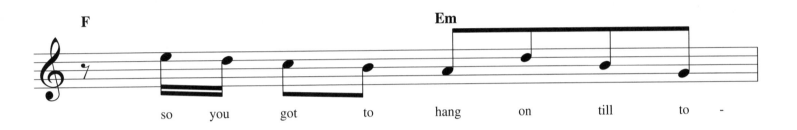

so you got to hang on till to -

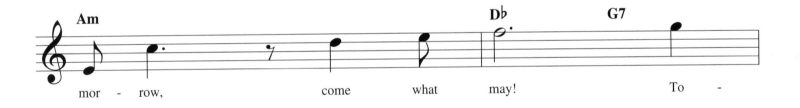

mor - row, come what may! To -

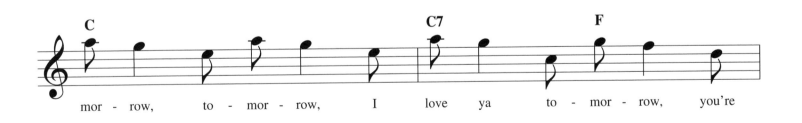

mor - row, to - mor - row, I love ya to - mor - row, you're

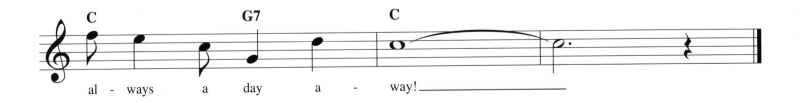

al - ways a day a - way!_____

TWINKLE, TWINKLE LITTLE STAR

Traditional

Gently

Twin - kle,   twin - kle,   lit - tle   star;

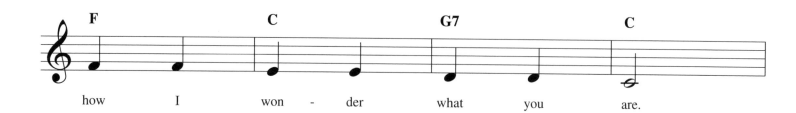

how   I   won - der   what   you   are.

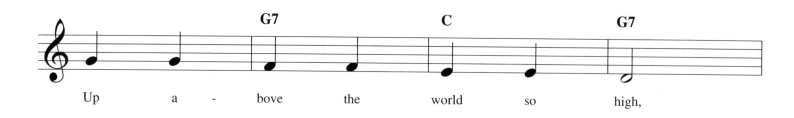

Up   a - bove   the   world   so   high,

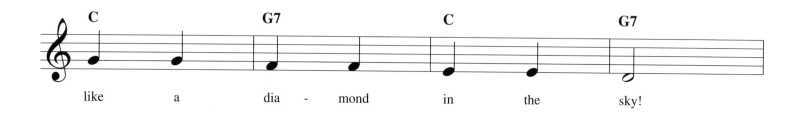

like   a   dia - mond   in   the   sky!

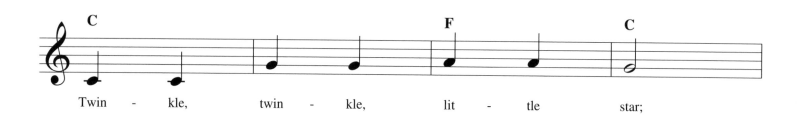

Twin - kle,   twin - kle,   lit - tle   star;

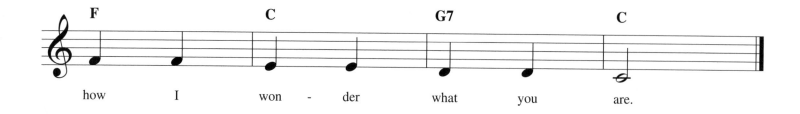

how   I   won - der   what   you   are.

WHEN THE SAINTS GO MARCHING IN

Words by KATHERINE E. PURVIS
Music by JAMES M. BLACK

Moderately fast

1. Oh, when the (5.) saints _____ go march - ing in, _____
2. sun _____ re - fuse to shine, _____
3. stars _____ have dis - ap - peared, _____
4. day _____ of judg - ment comes, _____

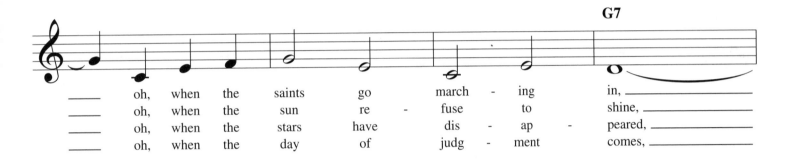

_____ oh, when the saints go march - ing in, _____
_____ oh, when the sun re - fuse to shine, _____
_____ oh, when the stars have dis - ap - peared, _____
_____ oh, when the day of judg - ment comes, _____

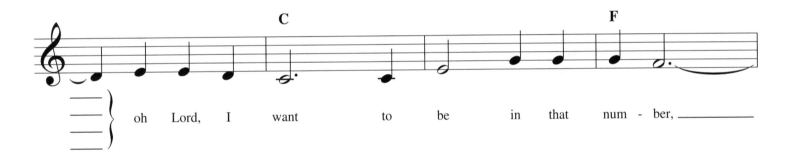

oh Lord, I want to be in that num - ber, _____

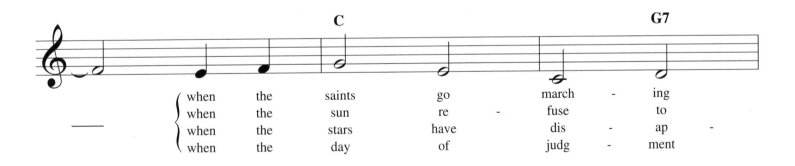

when the saints go march - ing
when the sun re - fuse to
when the stars have dis - ap -
when the day of judg - ment

1–4

in. _____
shine. _____
peared. _____
comes. _____

5

Oh, when the in. _____

THE UNBIRTHDAY SONG
from Walt Disney's ALICE IN WONDERLAND

Words and Music by MACK DAVID,
AL HOFFMAN and JERRY LIVINGSTON

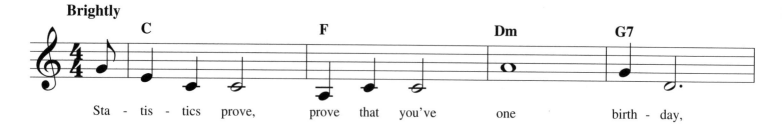

Sta - tis - tics prove, prove that you've one birth - day,

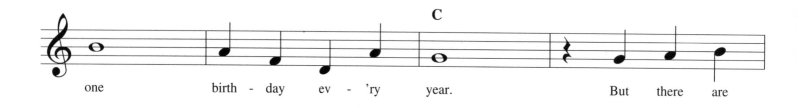

one birth - day ev - 'ry year. But there are

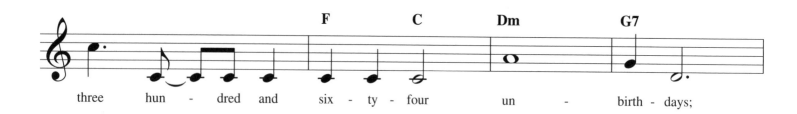

three hun - dred and six - ty - four un - birth - days;

that is why we're gath - ered here to cheer. _____ A

ver - y mer - ry un - birth - day to { you, to you. / me, to who? } A

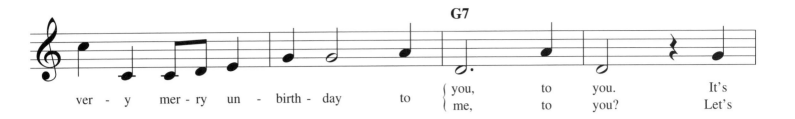

ver - y mer - ry un - birth - day to { you,   to   you.   It's
                                      { me,   to   you?   Let's

great   to drink to   some - one   and   I   guess that   you   will   do.
all   con - grat - u - late   me   with   a   pres - ent   I   a - gree.
                                                                        A

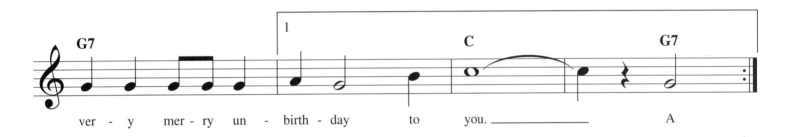

ver - y   mer - ry   un - birth - day   to   you. _____   A

birth - day,   a   ver - y   mer - ry   un - birth - day,   a   ver - ry   mer - ry   un -

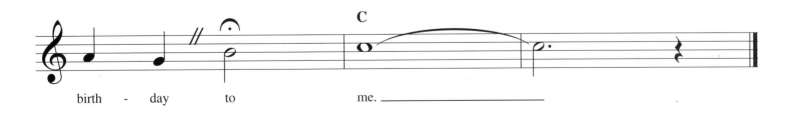

birth - day   to   me. _____

WINNIE THE POOH
from Walt Disney's THE MANY ADVENTURES OF WINNIE THE POOH

Words and Music by RICHARD M. SHERMAN
and ROBERT B. SHERMAN

YANKEE DOODLE

Traditional

Moderately fast

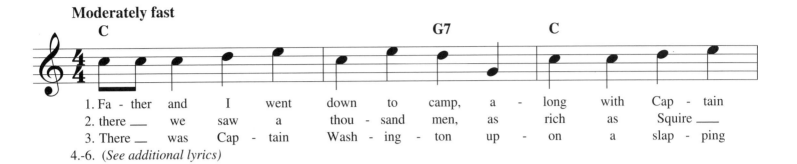

1. Fa - ther and I went down to camp, a - long with Cap - tain
2. there ___ we saw a thou - sand men, as rich as Squire ___
3. There ___ was Cap - tain Wash - ing - ton up - on a slap - ping

4.-6. (*See additional lyrics*)

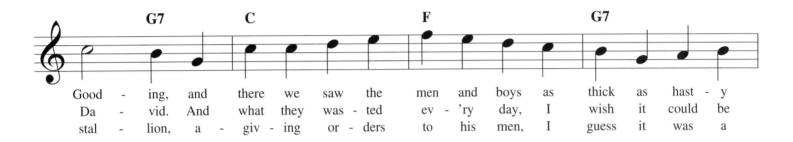

Good - ing, and there we saw the men and boys as thick as hast - y
Da - vid. And what they was - ted ev - 'ry day, I wish it could be
stal - lion, a - giv - ing or - ders to his men, I guess it was a

pud - ding.)
saved. ___ } Yan - kee Doo - dle, keep it up, Yan - kee Doo - dle dan - dy. Mind the mu - sic
mil - lion.)

and the step, and with the girls be hand - y. { 2.,4.,6. And hand - y.
5. We

Additional Lyrics

4. And then the feathers on his hat,
   They looked so 'tarnel fine, ah!
   I wanted peskily to get
   To give to me Jemima.

5. We saw a little barrel, too,
   The heads were made of leather.
   They knocked on it with little clubs
   And called the folks together.

6. And there they'd fife away like fun,
   And play on cornstalk fiddles.
   And some had ribbons red as blood
   All bound around their middles.

WON'T YOU BE MY NEIGHBOR?
(It's a Beautiful Day in the Neighborhood)
from MISTER ROGERS' NEIGHBORHOOD

Words and Music by
FRED ROGERS

Rhythmically

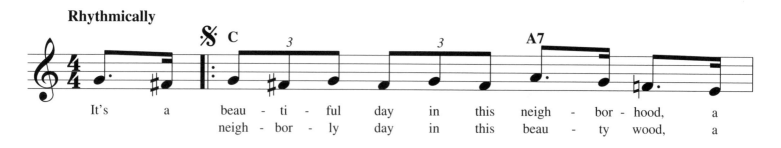

It's a beau-ti-ful day in this neigh-bor-hood, a
neigh-bor-ly day in this beau-ty wood, a

beau-ti-ful day for a neigh-bor. Would you be mine? ___ Could you
neigh-bor-ly day for a beau-ty. Would you be mine? ___ Could you

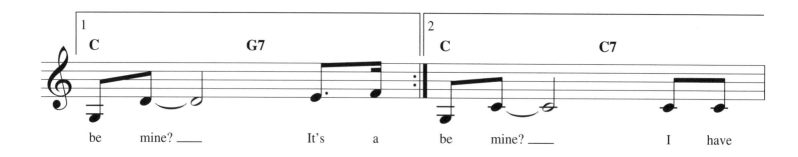

be mine? ___ It's a
be mine? ___ I have

al-ways want-ed to have a neigh-bor just like you! ___ I've

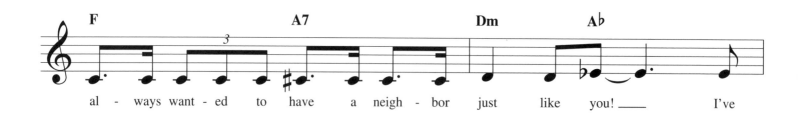

al-ways want-ed to live in a neigh-bor-hood with you. ___ So

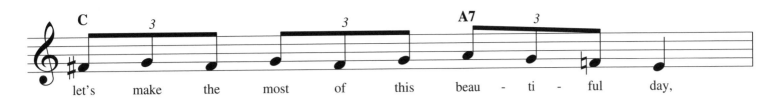

let's make the most of this beau - ti - ful day,

since we're to - geth - er we might as well say:

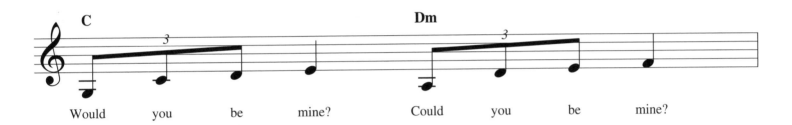

Would you be mine? Could you be mine?

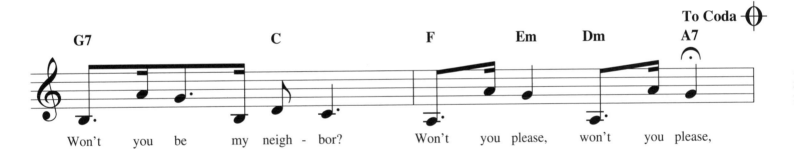

Won't you be my neigh - bor? Won't you please, won't you please,

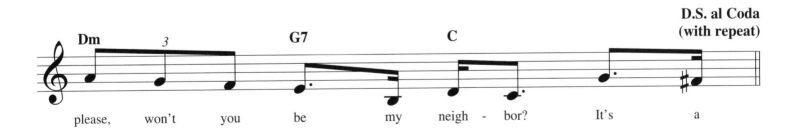

please, won't you be my neigh - bor? It's a

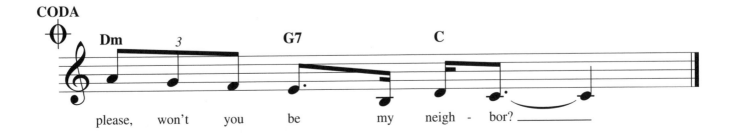

please, won't you be my neigh - bor?

YELLOW SUBMARINE

Words and Music by JOHN LENNON
and PAUL McCARTNEY

March tempo

In the town _____ where I was born lived a man _____ who sailed the

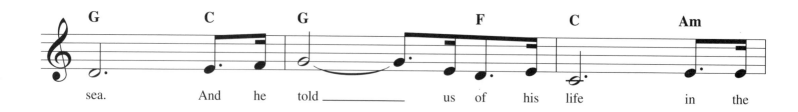

sea. And he told _____ us of his life in the

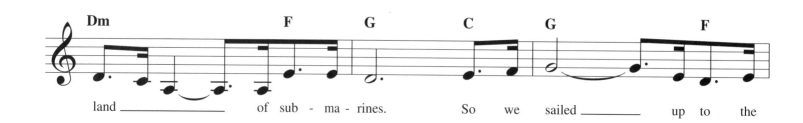

land _____ of sub - ma - rines. So we sailed _____ up to the

sun till we found _____ the sea of green. And we

lived _____ be-neath the waves in our Yel - low Sub - ma - rine.

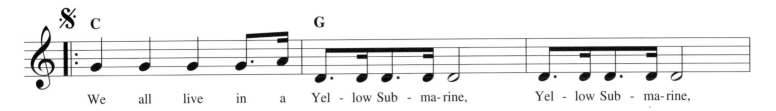

We all live in a Yel - low Sub - ma - rine, Yel - low Sub - ma - rine,

Yel - low Sub - ma - rine. We all live in a Yel - low Sub - ma - rine,

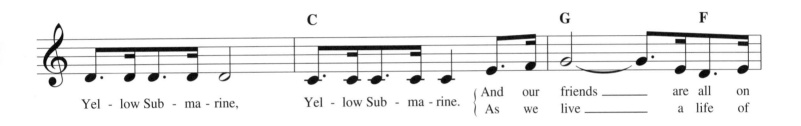

Yel - low Sub - ma - rine, Yel - low Sub - ma - rine. And our friends _____ are all on / As we live _____ a life of

board, man - y more of them live next door. And the band _____ be - gins to
ease, ev - 'ry one of us has all we need. Sky of blue _____ and sea of

play: *(Instrumental)*

green in our Yel - low Sub - ma - rine.

YOU ARE MY SUNSHINE

Words and Music by
JIMMIE DAVIS

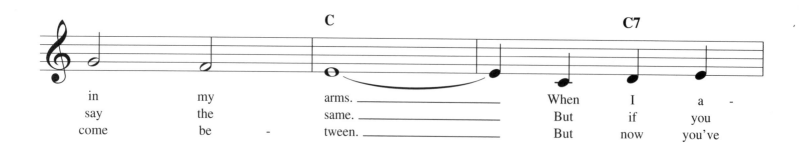

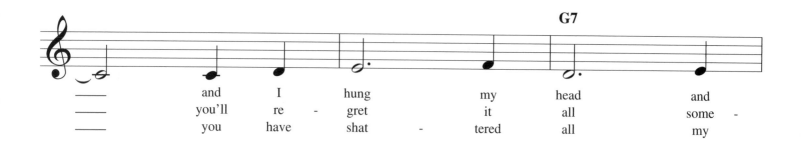

cried: \
day: \
dreams: \
You are my sun - shine, _____

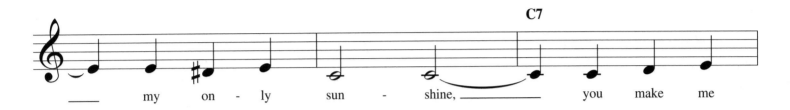

_____ my on - ly sun - shine, _____ you make me

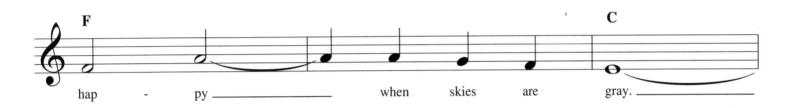

hap - py _____ when skies are gray. _____

_____ You'll nev - er know, dear, _____ how much I

love you. _____ Please don't take my sun - shine a -

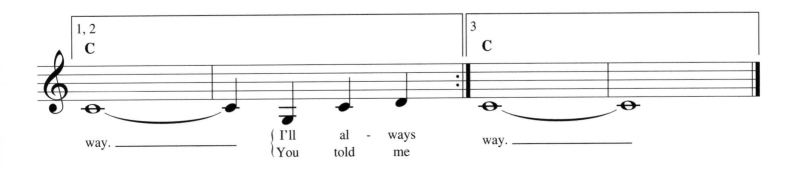

way. _____ I'll al - ways \
You told me \
way. _____

YOU CAN FLY! YOU CAN FLY! YOU CAN FLY!
from Walt Disney's PETER PAN

Words by SAMMY CAHN
Music by SAMMY FAIN

ZACCHAEUS

Traditional

Moderately

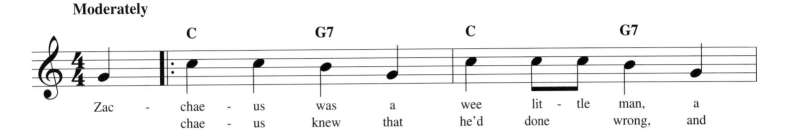

Zac - chae - us was a wee lit - tle man, a
chae - us knew that he'd done wrong, and

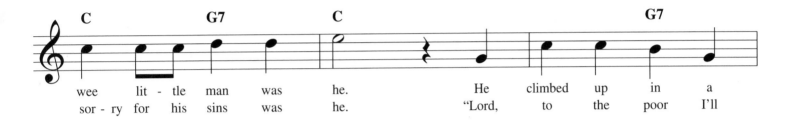

wee lit - tle man was he. He climbed up in a
sor - ry for his sins was he. "Lord, to the poor I'll

syc - a - more tree, for the Lord he want - ed to see. And
give one half of all my goods," said he. "And

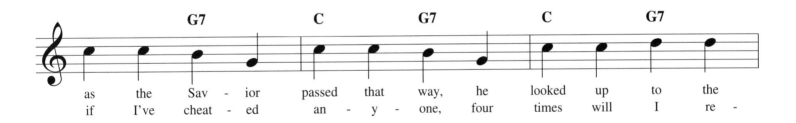

as the Sav - ior passed that way, he looked up to the
if I've cheat - ed an - y - one, four times will I re -

tree, *and He said, "Zacchaeus, you come down,* for I'm go - ing to your house to -
pay." *And Jesus said, "Salvation has come to you!* I have come to seek and

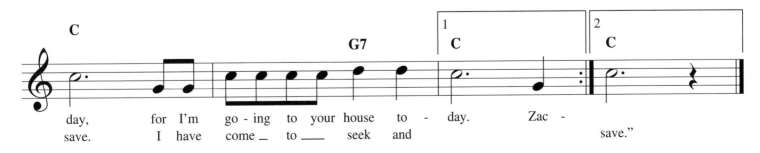

day, for I'm go - ing to your house to - day. Zac -
save. I have come to seek and save."

YOU'VE GOT A FRIEND IN ME
from Walt Disney's TOY STORY

Music and Lyrics by
RANDY NEWMAN

Easy Shuffle

You've got a friend in me. ____
You've got a friend in me. ____
You've got a friend in me. __
You've got a friend in me. __

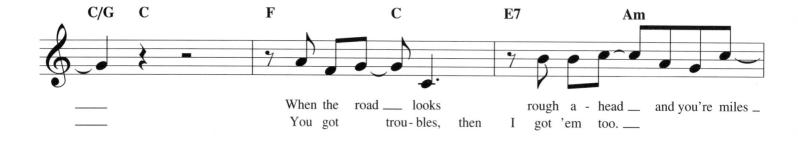

____
When the road ____ looks rough a - head __ and you're miles __
You got trou - bles, then I got 'em too. __

_____ and miles __ from your nice ____ warm bed, ____ you just re - mem - ber what your
There is - n't an - y - thing I would - n't do for you. If we stick to - geth - er we can

old pal said. ____ Son,
see it through, _'cause } you've ____ got a friend in me. _____ Yeah, you've __

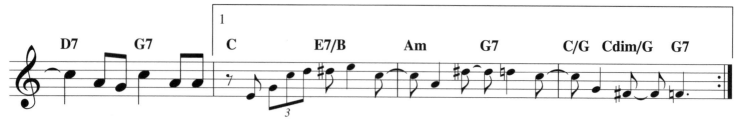

1

____ got a friend in me. *(Instrumental)*

2

Now, some oth - er folks might be a lit - tle bit smart - er than I am,

big-ger and strong - er too. ____ May - be. But none of them will

ev - er love ____ you the way ____ I do, ____ just me and you, ____ boy.

And as the years go by, ____ our friend-ship will nev - er die. __

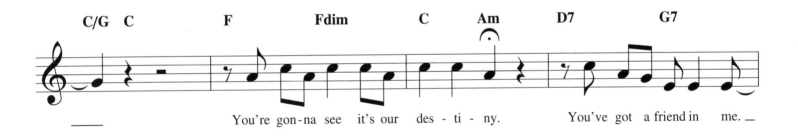

____ You're gon-na see it's our des - ti - ny. You've got a friend in me. __

____ You've got a friend in me. ____ You've got a friend in me. __

____ *(Instrumental)*

ZIP-A-DEE-DOO-DAH
from Walt Disney's SONG OF THE SOUTH
from Disneyland and Walt Disney World's SPLASH MOUNTAIN

Words by RAY GILBERT
Music by ALLIE WRUBEL

Brightly

Zip - a - dee - doo - dah,   Zip - a - dee - ay, _____

_____   my,   oh   my, _____ what   a

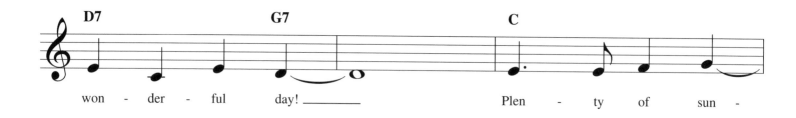

won - der - ful   day! _____   Plen - ty   of   sun -

- shine,   head - in'   my   way, _____

Zip - a - dee - doo - dah,   Zip - a - dee - ay! _____

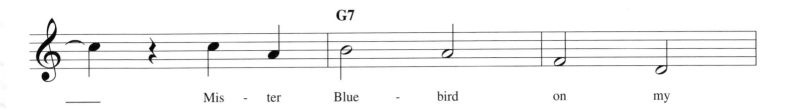

Mis - ter Blue - bird on my

shoul - der, _____ it's the truth it's

"act - ch'll," ev - 'ry - thing is "sat - is - fact - ch'll."

Zip - a - dee - doo - dah, Zip - a - dee - ay! ____

____ Won - der - ful feel - ing,

won - der - ful day. ____

CHORD SPELLER

C chords

C	C–E–G
Cm	C–E♭–G
C7	C–E–G–B♭
Cdim	C–E♭–G♭
C+	C–E–G♯

C♯ or D♭ chords

C♯	C♯–F–G♯
C♯m	C♯–E–G♯
C♯7	C♯–F– G♯–B
C♯dim	C♯–E–G
C♯+	C♯–F–A

D chords

D	D–F♯–A
Dm	D–F–A
D7	D–F♯–A–C
Ddim	D–F–A♭
D+	D–F♯–A♯

E♭ chords

E♭	E♭–G–B♭
E♭m	E♭–G♭–B♭
E♭7	E♭–G–B♭–D♭
E♭dim	E♭–G♭–A
E♭+	E♭–G–B

E chords

E	E–G♯–B
Em	E–G–B
E7	E–G♯–B–D
Edim	E–G–B♭
E+	E–G♯–C

F chords

F	F–A–C
Fm	F–A♭–C
F7	F–A–C–E♭
Fdim	F–A♭–B
F+	F–A–C♯

F♯ or G♭ chords

F♯	F♯–A♯–C♯
F♯m	F♯–A–C♯
F♯7	F♯–A♯–C♯–E
F♯dim	F♯–A–C
F♯+	F♯–A♯–D

G chords

G	G–B–D
Gm	G–B♭–D
G7	G–B–D–F
Gdim	G–B♭–D♭
G+	G–B–D♯

G♯ or A♭ chords

A♭	A♭–C–E♭
A♭m	A♭–B–E♭
A♭7	A♭–C–E♭–G♭
A♭dim	A♭–B–D
A♭+	A♭–C–E

A chords

A	A–C♯–E
Am	A–C–E
A7	A–C♯–E–G
Adim	A–C–E♭
A+	A–C♯–F

B♭ chords

B♭	B♭–D–F
B♭m	B♭–D♭–F
B♭7	B♭–D–F–A♭
B♭dim	B♭–D♭–E
B♭+	B♭–D–F♯

B chords

B	B–D♯–F♯
Bm	B–D–F♯
B7	B–D♯–F♯–A
Bdim	B–D–F
B+	B–D♯–G

Important Note: A slash chord (C/E, G/B) tells you that a certain bass note is to be played under a particular harmony. In the case of C/E, the chord is C and the bass note is E.